ABOVE: FEDERAL SOLDIERS POSE WITH A CAPTURED BIAFRAN PLANE AFTER RECLAIMING PORT HARCOURT, MAY 1968. BELOW: THE HYKKERS (LEFT TO RIGHT) JAKE SOLLO, EMMA LAWSON, PAT FINN, JEFF AFAM, IFY JERRY. 1971.

PART ONE

ROCK IN THE WAKE OF WAR

COMING BACK FROM HELL

After the war, something seemed different.

The Nigerian Civil War came to an end in January 1970. After thirty months of internecine combat, an estimated three million dead and the country almost torn apart spiritually and geographically, peace was finally back. Weapons were dropped, wounds were salved, and Nigeria was once again what it had been before: the Giant of Africa, a federation of diverse states, one nation bound in freedom, peace and unity. Head of State Yakubu Gowon magnanimously declared that the war had ended with "no victor and no vanquished," prohibiting all punitive actions or reprisals against the indigenes of the country's Eastern Region who had attempted to secede as the renegade Republic of Biafra. All Nigerians were urged to return to whatever they were doing before July 1967, forget the destruction and the bloodshed that had just transpired, and get back to the lives they had lived before the world went all to hell.

One of the more encouraging signs of a resumption of normalcy was the Hykkers' return to Lagos. As Nigeria's first professional pop group, the band had been a favorite among young groovers in the national capital in the carefree days of the mid 1960s, an era already taking on the hazy sepia tint of nostalgia. In the popular memory, the Hykkers' disappearance from Lagos coincided with the outbreak of war and symbolically signaled the end of the Good Old Days. Now the Hykkers were back, God was in His Heaven, happy days were here again.

But somehow it seemed different.

Lead singer Pat Finn was there, still as handsome as everyone remembered. So were dapper guitarist Jeff Afam and drummer Emmanuel Lawson. Bespectacled lead guitarist Bob Miga and bassist Eddie Duke were conspicuously missing, though, replaced by some new, younger boys who appeared noticeably rougher around the edges. But that wasn't the biggest change.

In some subtle, barely perceptible manner, it was apparent that the innocence was gone. The Hykkers — the clean-cut, grinning lads who once were Lagos' answer to the pre-*Revolver* Fab Four — appeared hard-bitten and surly. Gone were jangly guitars and bright harmonies; their sound was now rugged and murky, pulsing with the threat of barely-contained violence. Guitars screeched like low-flying fighter jets, basslines thrummed like trundling tank tracks. This was new music filled with funk, fuzz and fury. It was a sound that reflected a new, darker reality scarred by war, a forceful reminder to its audience that no matter how they might try to act like the preceding thirty months had never happened, they really would never be able to go home again.

The Hykkers had started out jamming together in late 1963, barely considering themselves a real band. They were just a revolving crew of young office workers and students having fun, crawling across the city, playing the latest Merseybeat hits that were popular with the younger generation, barely taken seriously in the highlife-dominated nightlife economy. "We would walk from club to club all night," says early member Harry Juwe. "This was when the streets of Lagos were safe at night. We would be just walking — hiking — all night. When they asked us our name, we didn't even have one... So we just said 'We are the Hykkers.'"

The Hykkers became a sensation as the group that finally took the beat subculture out of the afternoon teen hangouts into the world of mainstream Nigerian entertainment. By January 1965, the Hykkers had become TV stars, featuring regularly on the youth-centered weekly variety program *Saturday Square*. "Originally [the show's producers] had wanted our group to be called the Saturday Squares," Juwe remembers, "but we didn't like that. We didn't want our name to be so connected to the program, plus we were already becoming somewhat known as the Hykkers and so we saw no cause to change that."

Despite their protestations that they were amateurs, playing for the fun of it, the regular TV exposure thrust the unwitting youngsters toward professionalism: they scored the opening spot for Jamaican pop star Millie Small on a national tour in 1966. Millie's backing band was the new-wave highlife-jazz combo Fela Ransome-Kuti and his Koola

ABOVE: THE PRE-WAR HYKKERS, (LEFT TO RIGHT) FELIX UMOFFIA, JEFF AFAM, PAT FINN, BOB MIGA. CIRCA 1966. BELOW: UNIDENTIFIED POP GROUP, LAGOS. MID 1960S.

Lobitos. "Fela loved us so much that he told us that he was going to give us five horns," Finn says. "With those horns, our sound changed, it became so BIG and LOUD. It was so impressive that some representatives for a nightclub in Port Harcourt called Scorpidoo approached us after the show and said they wanted us to sign an exclusive contract." The band decamped eastwards to Port Harcourt in January 1967 for that upscale, modern cabaret, which catered to the considerable American and European expatriate community in the country's crude-producing Eastern region.

The announcement of the Hykkers' contract was cause for much celebration in the beat community. "It was a big deal," says Finn. "Because when we signed that contract, we became the first professional rock group in Nigeria. We were the first group that was getting paid to play, and getting paid well! They were paying us £700 a month, which was a huge amount of money." The Hykkers' abrupt exit from Lagos left a raft of bands vying for their vacated spot at the top of the pop pyramid, with the polished and highly professional Clusters emerging as the clear frontrunner. But the act that would next define the Lagos scene, however briefly, was the four-man Fractions, who had grabbed the spotlight in early 1967 after supporting the visiting Chubby Checker. Where the Hykkers had drawn most of their inspiration from Swinging London, the Fractions favored dirtier American R&B and the new sound called "soul." "We had been playing the Tamla-Motown sound, and we were the first group to introduce that in Lagos," remembers Fractions bassist Cliff Agwaze. "One day I heard a record at my neighbor's house. The song was called 'Papa's Got a Brand New Bag.' That blew my mind! It changed the way we thought about music."

The Fractions' James Brown-inspired sound, it turned out, was deep enough to change the way a lot of people in Lagos thought about music, as soul fever slowly started to spread across the city and infiltrate grown-up nightlife in a way that the beat wave never did. While the English beat sound was largely viewed as a juvenile trifle best suited to distract bored teenagers at afterschool boys and girls clubs, soul actually swept the nightclub scene and started to eclipse highlife in popularity, with patrons demanding that the highlife orchestras play recent hits by Otis Redding, Wilson Pickett, Eddie Floyd and Ray Charles.

But while soul's message of black solidarity was appealing to the music-loving public, on a larger scale the unity of the new Nigerian nation was in real peril: intense political rivalry between the Northern, Western and Eastern regions of the country led to ethnic riots in the North and West in which tens of thousands of Easterners were massacred. The Federal government's sluggish response to the pogroms had prompted the governor of the Eastern Region, Lt. Chukwuemeka Ojukwu, to call all Eastern indigenes across the country to return home to the safety of the Eastern region, which he declared was breaking away from Nigeria as the sovereign Republic of Biafra. This was in June 1967; by July, the country would be embroiled in civil war.

HYKKING THERE (AND BACK AGAIN)

The war had an immediate impact on the Lagos music scene—most of the major highlife bandleaders and musicians were of Eastern origin, and their mass defection from the capital drove the final nail into the coffin of highlife's embattled status as Nigeria's national music. The pop scene also suffered — with the Fractions amongst dozens of groups who quit Lagos to move back East — but enough soul groups emerged in the wake of the Eastern exodus to fill the void and keep Lagos jumping, as Nigeria went to war with Biafra to reclaim the country's oil-producing region. Chief among these was a new group called the Soul Assembly, fronted by singer Segun Bucknor. The Soul Assembly's presentation was sharp and exciting enough to land a recording contract, and they became the first act to release a record on Polydor's Nigerian subsidiary.

At the same time, Tony Benson was firmly establishing himself as Lagos's new Prince of Soul. The son of Nigerian showbiz pioneer Bobby Benson, Tony had cut his teeth as a multi-instrumentalist in his father's act and later as the Hykkers' drummer. Bobby Benson had not permitted Tony to follow the Hykkers to the East but instead installed him as the star act in his popular nightclub Caban Bamboo. On a special weekly "Soul Night," Tony thrilled crowds with his new band, the Combo. Soon, all of the remaining dance bands in the

ABOVE: THE PRE-WAR HYKKERS (LEFT TO RIGHT) EMMA LAWSON, PAT FINN, JEFF AFAM, BOB MIGA. CIRCA 1966. BELOW: SEGUN BUCKNOR OF THE SOUL ASSEMBLY. 1969.

city found themselves shifting the bulk of their repertoire from highlife to soul in order to retain their fan base.

Meanwhile, the Fractions arrived in Biafra with an incomplete roster—both bassist Agwaze and guitarist Sonny Okosun had been denied entry into the secessionist state since neither was of Eastern origin. The Biafran capital city of Enugu had its own nascent pop scene, with the top band in the city—the Postmen—having achieved what the vast majority of Lagos beats had been unable to: the Postmen had cut records. With the help of an Australian friend named Bruce Beresford—at the time a young aspiring filmmaker working with the Nigerian Film Commission in Enugu (and still twenty years away from winning an Oscar for directing *Driving Miss Daisy*)—the Postmen independently recorded an EP's worth of songs, some of which Beresford featured in one of his early shorts. The Fractions grabbed Jeremiah Jiagbogu, known as "Ify Jerry," a gangling, nineteen year-old lead guitarist who had started off in the Postman before making the rounds of other R&B bands in Enugu, and his partner Nkem "Jake Sollo" Okonkwo, himself a talented guitarist, for the bass. In no time at all, the Fractions were exploding, just as Nigeria and Biafra went to war.

"The Fractions became the biggest group in Biafra," remembers Chyke Madu, who played drums in the Biafran pop group the Figures. "They had brought a kind of energy and excitement to the stage. And they had a great manager, Tony Amadi, who promoted them so well that even in the middle of the war, when there was so much scarcity of everything, large crowds still paid good money to see the Fractions. They gave the Hykkers serious competition then."

Meanwhile, the Hykkers, for the first time in their tenure as a band, found themselves struggling. As the conflict escalated, the oil corporations withdrew their personnel from the area, and the Scorpidoo deal ended. With Biafra's borders blockaded, the Hykkers were unable to return to Lagos. Trapped in Biafra without the benefit of their cushy nightclub residency, they had to hustle for gigs, and for significantly reduced wages. Thanks to their esteemed reputation as national television stars, the Biafran government favored the Hykkers for propaganda purposes, which kept them a step or two ahead of the Fractions' assault as the war raged into 1968 and continued unabated into 1969.

By January 1970, however, it was clear that the Biafran resistance was crumbling. Millions of Biafrans fled the cities to escape the conquering Nigerian army, the Hykkers among them. Finally, the group was captured by the Nigerian forces, who were tickled to find the long-lost stars of *Saturday Square* hiding in the remote bush. The army commandeered the band to entertain the victorious troops as the war ended. But the Hykkers were restless to return to Lagos to resume the lives they had left before the war.

It was agreed amongst most of the group that their primary goal should be to escape the clutches of the army—and then immediately return to Lagos. However Miga, the group's unofficial leader, had a different view: his family had relocated to the East and he wanted to stay close to them. "This is where Bob Miga betrayed us," Finn says. "He went and informed the division commander of our plans to abscond. So the soldiers came and seized all our musical instruments. They said we can go if we want to, but we are not taking any instruments with us."

The Hykkers decided to leave anyway; Miga and bass player Eddie Duke were commissioned by the army to take the confiscated instruments and assemble a group to replace the departing Hykkers. With a few young recruits from the local soul group the Admirals, they formed a new band: the Strangers.

The Hykkers thus arrived in Lagos in early 1970 with no lead guitarist and no bassist. But fortunately for them their arch-rivals the Fractions had disintegrated in the last days of the war, freeing up the group's explosive guitar-and-bass duo, Ify Jerry and Jake Sollo. But the group still had no instruments, no money and no prospects.

"We were in Lagos for months before we could even get organized enough to start playing again," Finn says. "Eventually, it was our friend Fela who agreed to let us use his instruments to play." Fela Ransome-Kuti himself had just returned to Lagos from a mishap-ridden, ten-month U.S. tour, which nevertheless had an evident regenerative effect on him. Fela had always been considered a high-minded oddball on the highlife circuit; in the late 1960s he had announced that he was turning his back on highlife to focus on "Afro Beat," as he had dubbed his ambitious fusion of highlife, big-band Latin jazz and R&B. Fela's sophisticated Afro Beat arrangements had proven too

THE STRANGERS OF OWERRI. TOP ROW (LEFT TO RIGHT) SAM MCKING, JOE ARUKWE, GAB ZANI. BOTTOM ROW (LEFT TO RIGHT) ANII HOFNAR, BOB MIGA, GOGO BROWN. 1972.

FELA AT THE AFRIKA SHRINE. 1978.

dense, too busy, too *heavy* for crowds prepared to sway to the leisurely meter of highlife. But in the new soul epoch, the sound of Afro Beat made sense. Furthermore, Fela had stripped down his frantic horn charts to reveal a leaner, punchier, groove-based sound that fit in perfectly with the aggressive tone of soul and rock.

THE BIRTH OF AFRO ROCK

Meanwhile, the reborn Hykkers were bringing the Biafran sound to Lagos for the first time, with a unique new "Afro Rock" twist, powered primarily by Ify Jerry and Jake Sollo, a duo whose rhythmic brotherhood was undercut by a razorblade of competitive tension. "You could hear them always trying to out-do each other when we played," says Finn. "They were roommates too, and they were always fighting! When you go to their apartment, you would see everything in the room broken and scattered everywhere from the fighting."

The Fela/Hykkers double act became the hottest, hippest ticket in town, and soon expanded to include the Immortals, a dynamic soul group from Benin City, and Paperback Limited, a new Afro Rock outfit fronted by ex-Fraction Sonny Okosun. (These bands soon became known informally as Fela's "Afro Family," a movement their patriarch viewed as transformative in the musical and social landscape of Nigeria.) But the Afro Family was not the only new music movement taking flight in Lagos. Fela's friend Ginger Baker, drummer of the disbanded London rock trio Cream, had moved to town and set up shop at the Batakoto night club, where he hosted jam sessions with members of the Clusters, by then rechristened the Afro Collection. Baker was working on building a modern recording studio in Lagos, ARC (later also a record label), as well as shooting a film – *Ginger Baker in Africa*—that would expose Nigeria's growing underground music scene in London. He lived in Lagos for approximately six years, in the throes of what he called Nigeria's "flower power era" in the *Beware of Mr. Baker* documentary, greeting Paul McCartney in his studio to record for *Band on the Run*, while releasing albums by the likes of the Rock Town Express.

The steady work allowed the Hykkers to ground themselves: they bought new instruments and freed themselves from their reliance on Fela; they released their first single, the thunderous "Deiyo Deiyo (Akpunlunwobi)" b/w "I Want a Break Thru'" on HMV, indicating that the group was serious about becoming a permanent feature of the music scene. But there were rifts in the group: On one side were the veteran Hykkers, the young professionals who had played music as a lark, by now in their early thirties and buckling under the mounting pressure of adult responsibility. On the other side, Ify Jerry and Jake Sollo were still in their early twenties and firmly dedicated to music and good times. The older Hykkers seemed not to understand or particularly like some of the "freakier" aspects of the new music culture and appeared less and less interested in performing. Pat Finn was the first to leave, hanging up his microphone to take a fulltime job as a television producer. Jeff Afam also wearied of the endless grind and hand-to-mouth subsistence of the musician's life and secured a decidedly square—but more stable—position in the corporate sector. But as the departed Hykkers grew up and ascended to the buttoned-down ranks of mainstream society, the group's young lions moved in the opposite direction, digging deeper into the psychedelic underground. Jake Sollo started hanging with Ginger Baker's clique while Ify Jerry fell in with OFO the Black Company, a visually outlandish rock septet groomed by the Hykkers' manager Eddie Roberts.

Increasingly, keeping the Hykkers going seemed like a chore from which few of its members derived joy. The tension came to a head in April 1972 when, after playing a show at Club Chicago in Lagos, the Hykkers stowed their gear at the club for the night and went home. The next morning, the club's staff opened up to find the instruments smashed to bits. In trying to piece together what could have transpired, the staffers recalled that Jake Sollo had come back to the club as they were closing up, claiming to have forgotten something and assuring that he would lock up behind him. A police investigation found that he had demolished the instruments himself and he was promptly arrested. Only the intervention of Sollo's parents — who traveled to Lagos from Enugu — and

"I WANT A BREAK THRU" BY THE HYKKERS, RELEASED IN 1972.

THE CEEJEBS ON STAGE IN CALABAR (LEFT TO RIGHT) SYLVESTER AKAISO, SOKI OHALE, CHARLES "EFFI" DUKE. EARLY 1970S.

Roberts' string-pulling (his father was a former police inspector) saved Sollo from a stint in prison. But how could an already splintered Hykkers regroup from such an incident? Band solidarity was at an all-time low, so it was decided that this was a good enough a sign as any that it was time for the Hykkers to venture off in separate directions.

Pat Finn professes ignorance of Sollo's exact motivations but offers a theory: "I know that he had recently gotten admission to the university to study music. I think since he knew that he was leaving the group, he wanted to make sure that the Hykkers didn't continue and become successful without him."

The Hykkers would live on: mostly with the man who bore the blame for the group's destruction. Even as Jake Sollo shortly moved on to join the Funkees and then the UK-based Afro Rock supergroup Osibisa, he remained the most enthusiastic cheerleader for the Hykkers legacy and re-recorded "Deiyo Deiyo" *twice* during his solo career in the late 1970s. Reuniting with Finn in 1981 to produce Finn's first (and only) solo LP, he floated the idea of reuniting the Hykkers.

"He was so happy to see me, and I was happy to be working with him too," Pat Finn laughs. "But there was no way I was going to agree to be part of something like that! Not after all that I had already been through with that group!" Wistfully, he adds: "The Hykkers was something we did in the past, and I am proud of it, but let the past stay in the past."

PART TWO

LABEL WARS AND THE AFRO ROCK EXPLOSION

EMI ROCKS

No single company contributed more to facilitating the new wave of post-Civil War youth music than EMI Records. Electric and Musical Industries Ltd. had been one of the first companies to explore recording in Africa in the 1930s, but by the time the commercial record market exploded during the glory days of highlife in the early 1960s, the company had fallen by the wayside, overtaken by Decca and Philips. One of the hindrances to EMI's Nigerian progress was its location in Jos, Northern Nigeria, far away from the action in the Western and Eastern parts of the country. EMI appeared content to concentrate largely on releasing licensed foreign pop music from abroad but, after moving to Lagos in 1967, it set about grabbing its piece of the pie, mostly by recording the kinds of music that the other labels had theretofore ignored.

By the late 1960s, the soul craze was heating up. Decca and Philips avoided recording beat groups in general, viewing the music as a foreign fad that lay outside of their agenda to record indigenous genres. In addition, the primary audience for this music was perceived to be teenagers — children — who didn't have the disposable income to buy records anyway. Desperate EMI, with fewer such reservations, started signing emerging acts to its Parlophone imprint. Fela Ransome-Kuti and his Koola Lobitos, whose beat-influenced highlife style had up until then been viewed as too extreme for the mainstream highlife market, were one such group. When soul music came into full bloom in 1969, Parlophone became the place for youth-oriented acts to look for a home. The label had significant clout amongst this particular cohort due to its reputation on the international stage. "EMI was the label of the Beatles," says Lasbrey Ojukwu, whose group the Semi-Colon recorded for the label in the 1970s. "That was very impressive to us, because that was the group all of us who were playing rock or pop looked up to. It was a point of pride to be able to say you were recording for the same label as the Beatles."

After the war, EMI discontinued Parlophone in Nigeria and began to concentrate on recording new artists for its HMV imprint, specifically on the HNS series, on which it released Fela's Afro Beat sides, as well as records by the Afro Family bands. However, it was almost by accident that EMI Nigeria made the decision to cultivate the local rock scene: It issued a licensed single —"Funky Funky (Parts 1&2)"—a vaguely "Afro"-sounding soul record by the British studio band the Mohawks. "Funky Funky" was an unexpected hit in Nigeria, particularly in the East where young groovers

EMI AND DECCA/AFRODISIA PRINT ADS, 1972.

"ONYE IJE" BY THE STRANGERS, RELEASED IN 1972.

who bought and danced to the record believed it had been produced by a Nigerian group. Taking this as an indication that actual Nigerian pop, rock and soul records could find an eager audience, EMI sent agents into the former Biafran territory to sign acts from the emerging postwar rock scene such as the Actions, the Hygrades, the Strangers, the Bayonets and the Funkees. The gambit paid off in spades in 1972 when "Love Rock" b/w "Onye Ije" by Bob Miga's Strangers became the fastest-selling single in Nigerian history, proving that a strong market did exist for Nigerian rock. EMI stuck closely to the plot for the next few years: the first long-playing album issued on EMI Nigeria was BLO's Afro Rock masterpiece *Chapter One*.

One of the key players in EMI's success was studio manager Odion Iruoje, who imbued the music with a uniquely local vision. Iruoje's background was in electronics, not music, but after he trained at EMI's Abbey Road Studios in 1969, around the time the Beatles were recording their classic *Abbey Road* LP with producer George Martin, he returned with advanced ideas of the album as more than a mere document of a live performance. Iruoje followed Martin's belief that the studio could be an instrument, and recordings deliberately constructed works of art. Iruoje's first major hit was Fela Ransome-Kuti's "Jeun K'oku," which succeeded in focusing Fela's ideas and delivering the explosive energy of his live shows where previous records had faltered. Almost overnight, Fela went from a niche taste to one of the hottest artists in Nigeria, and Iruoje went about the business of scouting the clubs for other obscure acts to turn into stars.

Iruoje was particular about the artists he chose to produce, looking for musical ability, an electrifying live performance and, above all, originality. At a time when most pop groups strived to sound as close as possible to their foreign inspirations, Iruoje wanted artists who had a uniquely Nigerian style, both in music and lyrics, often urging artists to mine their indigenous folklore and other local sources for material. "Odion did not like anybody who was playing copyright," says Ginger Forcha of the band Wrinkar Experience. "But if you were original, that was how you got his attention. That was the reason he wanted to record Wrinkar Experience, because we weren't copying anybody. We didn't sound like anybody else."

Wrinkar Experience was a band founded in 1971 by guitarist/organist Forcha and bassist Edjo'o Jacques Racine, both natives of Cameroon who had emigrated to Nigeria, attracted by its flourishing rock scene. After jamming with various Cameroonian and Nigerian musicians, the group coalesced with the addition of Nigerian singer-songwriter/lead guitarist Danie Ian and drummer Geoffrey Omadhebo, both prior members of Sonny Okosuns' Paperback Limited. Ian had a knack for penning catchy, articulate tunes, and when Iruoje caught the band playing at a nightclub, he couldn't believe that a Nigerian group could perform with such maturity and confidence. He immediately invited them to EMI Studios where they recorded a single featuring Ian's compositions "Fuel For Love" and "Soundway." When the record was released in late 1972, it outstripped the heights reached by "Love Rock," signaling that Nigerian rock had come to stay.

"Fuel for Love" was such a big hit that EMI could barely wait to get out another single from Wrinkar Experience. By this time, the company had outfitted its studio with a new 8-track recorder, and Iruoje was eager to try out the new equipment recording the label's premier rock band. Wrinkar and Iruoje recorded another of Ian's songs, "Money to Burn," but found themselves without another song suitable to include on the b-side. On the spot, Forcha conjured up a dark and mysterious groove from his native Bamileke folkways, just as Iruoje liked.

By this time, the group's membership was incomplete as drummer Omadhebo and rhythm guitarist Pierre Dzelezek had been poached by other bands. This shortcoming actually turned out to provide the perfect opportunity to explore the possibilities of the new multitrack recorder, with Ian playing rhythm guitar and then overdubbing sizzling lead runs, and Forcha vamping on organ and overdubbing coloratura played on a piccolo he had bought from a drunken English sailor the night before. The resulting record, "Ballad of a Sad Young Woman," sounds like a psychedelic soul-cry from another dimension, and effectively proved Iruoje's facility for creating sonically sophisticated studio recordings.

GINGER FORCHA OF WRINKAR EXPERIENCE, 1975

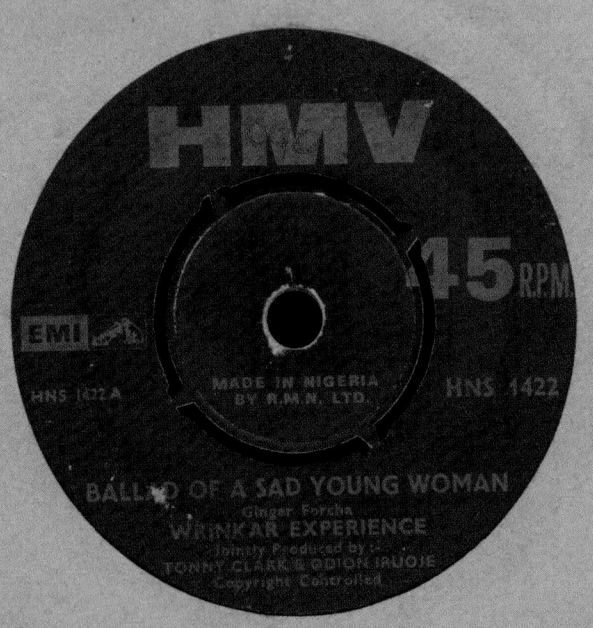

NIGERIAN BROADCASTING CORPORATION

AFRODISIA ASCENDS

"THE SUPREME RECORD." For many years this was the legend proudly emblazoned across the labels of discs issued by Decca Records UK. With reference to its interests in West Africa at least—and in Nigeria in particular—it was a boast substantiated by the company's regional track record. Decca jumpstarted the market for locally-recorded music with its bestselling West Africa series, launched in 1947. Decca was the first label to commit to installing studios in West Africa, breaking ground on professional recording facilities in Accra, Ghana and Lagos when other labels were still recording West African artists in makeshift closet and garage setups. Records adorned with Decca's bright yellow label were recognized for their startling fidelity, thanks to its patented "full-frequency range-recording" technology. Decca facilitated the profusion of the highlife genre in the 1950s via its legendary series of sides starring dance band highlife pioneer E.T. Mensah and his Tempos.

Without a doubt, the yellow Decca label was an emblem of distinction and every other record company vied for second place. This was the reality for nearly two decades—then came the 1970s. On the international level, the company's reputation had taken a bit of a drubbing in the previous decade, becoming a record industry punchline for passing on signing the Beatles. In Nigeria, Decca would register a missed opportunity in failing to recognize the soul music boom and it was outpaced by the Polydor imprint. Via groundbreaking releases by Segun Bucknor and the Soul Assembly, the Ibadan Garrison Organisation, Orlando Julius, and Fela Ransome-Kuti, Polydor established itself as the definitive home of cutting-edge youth music, the label that represented the coming of age of a new generation with new values, new tastes—and new disposable income. After the war, EMI's HMV label took the baton from Polydor and carried it to the next post: Decca found itself looking like the record company that would always be the also-ran.

The dipping trend of Decca's credibility was not lost on Dave Bennett, the managing director of its West Africa division, and he had an idea to return the company to the forefront of innovation with a rebranding, a rebirth. He ordered the creation of a new label focused on modish youth music, with a name and imagery that reflected the spirit of the times—Black consciousness, uninhibited sexuality, a laidback bohemian ethos and psychedelic fashion.

The first task was to establish a baseline. BLO, dissatisfied with EMI's release of their debut, sought help wherever they might find it (the first copy of *Chapter One* rediscovered in the West came with a note from BLO manager Tony Amadi addressed to Manticore Records expressing just this). Bennett quickly signed the band and issued their self-produced *Phase II* album. He then scouted Lagos's hottest nightclubs to find some fresh, exciting talent to sign. It was at a special showcase at Fela's Afrika Shrine that Bennett found a group that encapsulated everything that the new Decca must stand for. OFO the Black Company was loud, freaky, weird, theatrical and spiritual—an act the likes of which had never before been seen in Nigeria. Alongside BLO, they were the perfect band to restore Decca's stature as the steward of all things avant-garde. The new Afrodisia imprint would take inspiration from OFO's funky aesthetic.

OFO's 1972 debut on Afrodisia set things off on a promising note, scorching the radio waves and dance floors across the country. Afrodisia set out to capitalize on the success by signing more bands that could deliver intense rock in a similar mode—Cicada, Voices of Darkness, World Affairs, the Thermometers, the Kukumbas, "Blackman" Akeeb Kareem—and bands that found a more restrained approach, like the Formulars Dance Band, Godwin Ironbar, Soundscope Ltd and George Akaeze's Augmented Hits. Afrodisia's pink label soon became associated with high-frequency psych-pop or "native rock" (Afrodisia's preferred nomenclature over "Afro Rock") sounds — considerably brighter in texture than EMI's grungier aesthetic—and the label's standard production credit mentioned only Bennett.

Looking back on the early Afrodisia discography from today's vantage point, it presents a thrilling panorama of new wave Nigerian music from the early 1970s. But when compared to the catalogs of the other major labels from the same period, its breadth decreases. Artist and band names on records from EMI

ABOVE: FANS ROCKING OUT AT A CONCERT BY GHANAIAN BAND THE PSYCHEDELIC ALIENS IN LAGOS. 1970. BELOW: BLO'S BERKLEY JONES (LEFT) AND LAOLU AKINS (CENTER) WITH DECCA RECORDS' MANAGING DIRECTOR AND AFRODISIA PRODUCER DAVE BENNETT. 1973.

"WAKE UP YOU" BY WAVES, RELEASED IN 1973.

and Philips reappear throughout the decade, and some go beyond. Many of them would go on to achieve legendary stature in the annals of Nigerian music. However, most of those who managed to snag an Afrodisia catalog number show up once, maybe twice, and then are never heard from again, remembered neither by fans, the media, nor by industry professionals. This must be blamed on Afrodisia's nonchalant approach to artist development. EMI's policies in particular throw Afrodisia's deficiencies into stark relief: EMI had strong A&R agents both in Lagos and in the East, as well as an aggressive nationwide distribution network; Afrodisia was considerably weaker in both departments. While neither company was particularly generous in terms of doling out royalty payments, EMI had the advantage of being in the business of manufacturing and distributing musical instruments and electrical equipment, so it could offer artists performance gear in lieu of royalties. The label's stars might even be gifted the use of a bus, which allowed them to earn a living through touring, simultaneously building reputations that in turn fed record sales. By the mid 1970s, Afrodisia bled talent as artists fled to EMI.

An example of an act Afrodisia let down was the Waves, a heavy rock quartet hailed as Nigeria's most promising pop act in 1973. The Waves had started as a soul band in 1968, often playing with Don Bruce, "the James Brown of Lagos," but the group's members—lead guitarist April Laine, bassist Akuma Walters, rhythm guitarist Dave Kumalo and drummer Goddy Jasper—all loved Jimi Hendrix, Carlos Santana and Eric Clapton, and started to integrate screeching guitar work into their soul stew. The Waves were one of several Lagos rock and soul groups that migrated to Northern Nigeria to fill the void of groups to play in the burgeoning nightlife scene there. All, that is, except for Laine who stayed behind in Lagos to play guitar in the original lineup of Monomono before joining the Thermometers, with whom he recorded a single for Afrodisia.

The Waves returned to Lagos by 1972, transformed from their old soul schtick. "When the Waves came back, they had big afros and were wearing Islamic attire," says the musician known only as Micro Mike, of the late 1960s Lagos soul band the Sunflowers, and who also recorded for Afrodisia during this period. "They had a freaky look that made people want to check them out." With Laine back in the fold and drummer Eric Mann taking Jasper's place, the Waves earned an avid following amongst high school and college students, which convinced Decca they could be promoted as heirs to OFO. Laine recalls going to the Decca studio to record the single "Mother" b/w "Wake Up You," which he maintains was produced by the members of the group themselves, despite the credit given Bennett on the label. "He wasn't in the studio with us. We never met him, even when we were signing up with the label," Laine says of Bennett. "You know, back in those days a lot of people got credited as 'producer' even if they didn't do anything musical or technical on the record."

He continues: "The person who owns the label or runs the label calls himself the producer. The person who paid the money to sponsor the session is the producer. The person who maybe bought instruments for the band also wants to be called the producer. It was a formality, but it doesn't mean they really added something to the music itself. Everyone was just doing their own thing in the studio."

Ultimately, Laine believes that the group was too inexperienced to fully produce a record and too little was done on Afrodisia's part to produce a high-quality rock recording. "We weren't even happy with the way the final product sounded," he says. "The vocals could have been better." The record was dumped into the market with little fanfare from Afrodisia, despite some rave reviews by critics. The end result? "It didn't do so well," Laine says. "We didn't think that Decca promoted it at all, which is part of why we wanted to leave that label. So we had to break up Waves and re-form under the name Living Truth. We were a trio by then—myself, Akuma and Eric, without Dave. We signed up with EMI as Living Truth and we did some shows, but we broke up before we even recorded anything again."

Other artists followed the Waves' path toward EMI, many also changing their names to distance themselves from their underwhelming Afrodisia releases. Afrodisia seemed unconcerned, as it changed focus to cultivate cash

(LEFT TO RIGHT) GEOFFREY OMADHEBO AND GODDY JASPER OF THE CUTES (AND LATER THE WAVES). LATE 1960S.

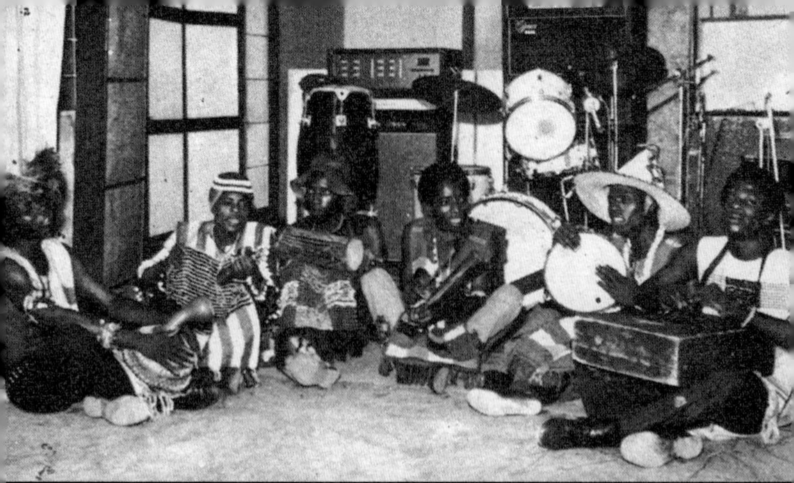

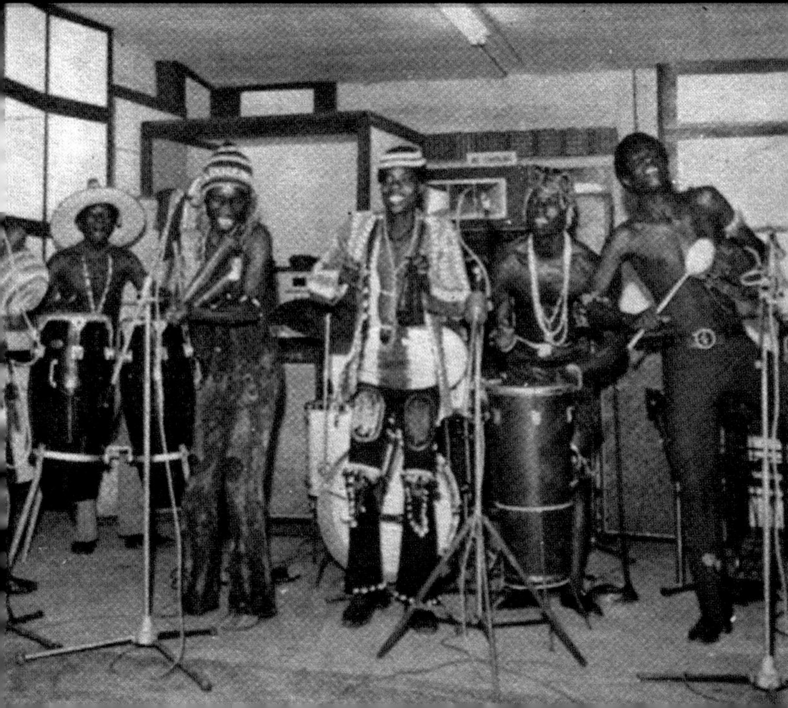

cows such as the Oriental Brothers, an Eastern guitar highlife group that remained among the top-selling artists in Nigeria into the early 1980s. By the mid 1970s, Afrodisia was fixated on luring Fela into the fold, signing him to a million-dollar, multi-album contract. The deal went bad, however, when Afrodisia hesitated to release several of the albums Fela delivered for fear that the records' anti-authoritarian content might invite the ire of the Nigerian government, which was already scrutinizing the activities of foreign corporations such as Decca. The resulting skirmish saw Fela vandalizing and shutting down the Decca office and turning public opinion against the company (including accusing it of being a front for the CIA). Decca withdrew its interests in Afrodisia by the end of the decade and left Nigeria altogether. Afrodisia continued to live on, though it never again would come close to fulfilling its promise as the music label on the edge of the Nigerian new.

OFO THE BLACK COMPANY'S ACID ROCK CULT

As the Hykkers came to the end of the road, Ify Jerry Jiagbogu kept moving: Eddie Roberts encouraged him to join the ranks of OFO the Black Company, undoubtedly the strangest band of musicians to ever emerge on the Nigerian music scene. The group was unconventional in its refusal to present itself as an entertainment ensemble with the attendant matching suits, coordinated stage moves and toothy showbiz grins. No, OFO was a "musical cult" with an image steeped in mysticism, stemming from its very name, which referenced *ofo*, a sacred staff that served amongst the Igbo people as a representation of ancestral authority and destiny, through its members' Afro-shamanic look. After an introduction, Ify Jerry found himself falling under the sway of OFO's "chief" (not leader, as every member was designated as equal), a charismatic musical conceptualist named Larry Ifedioranma Jr.

"Larry was just a... *different* kind of guy," Ify Jerry remembers. "He thought in a way that not a lot of people were thinking back then. He was into the pro-Black philosophy and all kinds of alternative spirituality that I didn't even understand at the time. I had no idea what he was talking about most of the time! All I cared about was music, and he was into the type of hard rock that I wanted to play." Ifedioranma's otherworldly progressivism, however, belied a considerably more conservative background than most would have assumed.

Born in 1949, Ifedioranma grew up in a large musical family headed by a stern pastor father. As a sophomore at the University of Ibadan in the late 1960s, he was recruited into the Nigerian Army to serve as a singer and drummer in the wildly popular Ibadan Garrison Organization band. But as Larry entertained in a group of straight-laced military musicians, trading off leads with co-vocalist "Blackman" Akeeb Kareem on highlife hits and James Brown- or Wilson Pickett-inspired soul numbers, he dreamed of reaching for the outer limits of contemporary music explored by the likes of Jimi Hendrix and Deep Purple. His ambition: the creation of Nigeria's first acid-rock band.

Ifedioranma's dream took a step towards reality when he hooked up with Ibadan Garrison Organization guitarist Benna Kemfa to form a "black underground rock" quintet called the Silent Man as a sub-group of the military band. "Nobody understood what we were up to," Ifedioranma explained to *Newbreed* magazine in 1973. "Our music was too far ahead of the people then, so they couldn't dig. We packed it up for lack of encouragement." After the war, when Ifedioranma and Kemfa were honorably discharged from the army, they decided to give the underground rock group concept another go. "Benna and I came over to Lagos still determined to work for God and mankind through our kind of music," Ifedioranma declared. "OFO the Black Company is therefore the result of our determination."

OFO made their first big splash at Fela's Afrika Shrine on a bill headlined by Ginger Baker & Salt. OFO's mishmash of music, mysticism and theater blew the main act off the stage. As the legend of OFO's performance reverberated across Lagos, Decca offered the group a deal. As a show of commitment to this vision of OFO as a standard-bearer for the bold, new Decca, the group was outfitted with state-of-the-art gear and its new youth-oriented imprint — that would be Afrodisia — was built around them, complete with a vignette of OFO guitarist Popo Kamson's girlfriend's afro-haloed head as the label's official insignia.

ABOVE: OFO'S LARRY IFEDIORANMA. EARLY 1980S. BELOW: OFO'S LARRY
IFEDIORANMA (CENTER) IN THE STUDIO WITH UNKNOWN OTHERS, 1980.

"BEAUTIFUL DADDY" BY OFO THE BLACK COMPANY, RELEASED IN 1972.

"EVERYBODY LIKES SOMETHING GOOD" BY IFY JERRY KRUSADE, RELEASED IN 1972.

IFY JERRY. 1971.

OFO the Black Company disappointed no one, delivering on their hype with their first single, "Allah Wakbarr," a screaming, proto-metal orgy of ecstasy exploding around the traditional Islamic exhortation of the creator's greatness. "It's not like Larry was even a Muslim," says Ify Jerry, who played keys on the record. "He was just into embracing all kinds of spirituality." (The group would later record "The Book," a companion piece to "Allah Wakbarr," exalting the wisdom of the Christian Bible.)

"Allah Wakbarr" was backed with "Beautiful Daddy," another slab of jam-heavy rock that opened with a simple organ statement by Ify Jerry. OFO was on its way, and so was Afrodisia.

IFY JERRY'S SOLO KRUSADE

When he joined OFO, one of the first things Jeremiah "Ify Jerry" Jiagbogu noticed was the group had an unusual bipartite structure. Under the umbrella of the Black Company existed a parallel group comprising chiefly Benna Kemfa, Popo Kamson, and percussionist Kinglsey "King UD" Obiche. Ify Jerry cast his lot with the splinter group. "I think the group was called Akamba," he says. "Anyway, it was the members of that group that played with me on my record."

The record in question is the single "Everybody Likes Something Good" b/w "Nwantinti/Die Die," credited to "Ify Jerry Krusade" and released on Polydor Records in 1972. Shortly after the success of "Allah Wakbarr," Ify Jerry abruptly walked away from Ifedioranma's swift-rising rock phenomenon. "My parents wanted me to come back home since I had been away for so long," Jerry explains. "So I left Lagos and went back to Enugu."

Back in Enugu, Ify Jerry floated around the music scene, sitting in with various bands and occasionally fronting a new, fluctuating lineup of the Krusade for a year before his parents shipped him off in 1974 to America, where he has remained. "I was one of the founders of the music scene after the war," he says. "But I ended up missing most of what came afterwards. A lot of the groups that became big later in the 1970s, I've never even heard of them."

OFO EXPLODES

Under manager Eddie Roberts' expert handling, OFO went from strength to strength. A second single on Afrodisia, "Love Is Me, Love Is You" b/w "Make Up Your Mind," kept the home front hot while Decca's release of "Allah Wakbarr" in the UK expanded their audience internationally. 1973 saw the Black Company selected to represent Nigeria at the 10th World Festival of Youth and Students in East Berlin. OFO the Black Company's psychedelic assault thrilled the festival audience and won the group a gold medal. Though perhaps the real prize was an anecdote Ifedioranma would trade for years thereafter: During OFO's set, one of the hippies in attendance asked if he could join the group onstage. In the spirit of love and sharing, Larry let the shaggy-haired stranger sit in on guitar for a few numbers and found that he enlivened the OFO sound with his hair-raising solos. Only after the set, when the mysterious guest had been hugged and bidden farewell did Larry realize OFO the Black Company's musical cult had briefly included Carlos Santana.

After that triumph it was onward west, to conquer the United Kingdom. "When I arrived in London, OFO had already been there for some months, and I desperately wanted to see them," says Dele Olaseinde, who left Nigeria to attend London Polytechnic in early 1974. Olaseinde was a veteran of the Lagos beat scene, having led the schoolboy quartet the Vampires in the mid 1960s before joining the Clusters. Now he was eager to reunite with OFO members Popo Kamson and Tokunbo Shotade, with whom he had played in a short-lived teenage rock n' roll combo. "I looked all over town for them for months before I finally found them playing at the Iroko Club at Haverstock Hill."

Located in the chic Hampstead area, the Iroko Country Club was a ballroom owned by Ginger Folorunso Johnson, a Nigerian percussionist and bandleader who had been a fixture of the London black music scene since the 1940s. He became a popular figure in the exotic "freak" fringes of Swinging London, and did well for himself, contributing to the scores of Tarzan films, the 007 installment *Live and Let Die*, and other movies. Johnson is frequently credited as a progenitor of Afro Rock, having crossbred bluesy electric guitars with African drumming in the mid 1960s and having shared the stage with the Rolling Stones on their 1969 *Stones in the Park* television special, his African group joyously throwing up a wall of percussion on "Sympathy for the Devil." The Iroko Club became a popular venue for Johnson's friends in the city's rock elite, amongst them Rod Stewart, Elton John, and Pink Floyd.

Olaseinde had heard that OFO was an eight-man band, but by the time he caught them at Iroko, they were a guitarless quartet featuring Ifedioranma on drums, his brother Dediga "Johnny" Ifedioranma on percussion, Soni Makoko on bass and Toks Shotade on organ.

"What I found strange was that after they played, as everybody was leaving the club to go home and the place was being closed, the members of the group were going back into the club," Olaseinde remembers. "So I followed them back in, and found out they were sleeping there in the club!"

Olaseinde soon learned that OFO's British sojourn had started out on a reassuring note, as Decca had installed the band in a comfortable farmhouse in Surrey, and they had won over the freaks in some energetic pub gigs. However, things soon went off course. Decca had little idea how to market an African heavy rock group to UK audiences, and worse yet, OFO's structural dichotomy had reached breaking point. "The group had split into two," Olaseinde explains. "On the one side you had Popo Kamson, Kemfa, Kingsley and Eddie Roberts. On the other side was Larry, Johnny, Toks, and Soni Makoko. Larry and them left the farmhouse and moved to London, while Popo's side stayed behind in Surrey. I think they were trying to organize themselves as an alternate version of the Black Company."

Ifedioranma's group—now known simply as OFO, due to his concern that "the Black Company" might be too racially alienating to the mainstream audience—had during this time managed to record "The Book" b/w "Let's Go Where the Action Is," produced by session guitarist Pip Williams, best known at the time for his work with glam-pop boy band the Sweet and smooth American doowoppers-cum-black rockers Bloodstone.

The record's gentle, quasi-tropical flavor, polite African choral chanting and loungey piano harmony represented a shocking castration of the elephantine power and quicksilver intensity that characterized "Allah Wakbarr"—suggesting that the label's vision for OFO was the same sphere of anodyne Afro-Exotica that Osibisa had begun to explore.

"OFO didn't have a guitarist at that time," Olaseinde says, "so Soni Makoko handed me a Guild electric guitar and I joined the group." With the addition of Olaseinde restoring the group's heretofore gelded heavyweight sound, they recorded the LP *OFO the Black Company* at Decca's Tollington Park, London studios in 1974. It appeared that the band was again on the rise, but elation became disappointment when they discovered that the album was being unceremoniously dumped in the Nigerian market without so much as a token European release.

Still lacking support from the label, OFO continued to play Iroko by night, both as a headlining act and as Ginger Johnson's backing band. "We would play at night," Olaseinde says. "In the morning, we would clear out the club for Thin Lizzy and other groups to use as a rehearsal space." The band also backed Johnson on an album recorded at Pye Studios. "We were flat broke," Olaseinde adds. Still, Olaseinde says, he and the others stuck it out, enthralled by Ifedioranma's passion, talent and conviction that the group was bound for major success. "Larry's creativity was just so inspiring. He would sit down with the guitar and play some chord progressions... I tell you, I still hear those chords in my head today and my mind is still blown."

Unfortunately, dissent crept in as Ifedioranma's drive propelled him into directions incongruous with the group's peace and love philosophy. "Larry and Ginger took a drive to Surrey with their henchmen," says Olaseinde. "They stormed the farmhouse with like six big West Indian guys, overpowered Eddie Roberts, Popo and the rest, and snatched the equipment they had there: guitars, Marshall amps... They took everything." OFO suffered another blow when Johnson died suddenly during a visit to Nigeria in July 1975, bringing an end to the band's tenure at the Iroko Club. With the loss of their benefactor and their home venue, the group played together less frequently, its members placing greater priority on scratching out a living from menial jobs. Olaseinde states that, at this time, "the group was psychologically splitting up."

Ifedioranma, however, never lost his momentum. He became convinced that the group's "blackness" was its fatal flaw, and a more racially integrated membership would remedy their woes. "Larry was trying to bring new members into the group," says Olaseinde. "He thought we could be more commercial if we distanced ourselves from the African thing, so he wanted to bring in some English girl he was dating as a singer, and her brother to play the drums. It didn't sound right. Without Larry on the drums, it just didn't sound like OFO... It sounded like any other rock group in Britain."

"Larry wanted a much heavier approach to the music," offers English guitarist Graham Gaffney, who had befriended Ifedioranma earlier in 1975. "He put the band's failure to maintain their African success in England down to their inability to compete dance-wise with the current charts." Gaffney was twenty years old, and had just been invited to join the 101ers — the London pub rock outfit that enjoyed a brief blush of regional popularity in the early 1970s. Impressed by Ifedioranma's steely focus and unfettered creativity, Gaffney turned down the 101ers gig and agreed to join a new OFO lineup: Ifedioranma on drums, Gaffney on guitar, Johnny on congas, Greg McLean on bass and a Jamaican percussionist known only by his first name, Keith. In the meantime, the current version of the group secured a very welcome spot opening for reggae star Desmond Dekker at a campus concert.

"Goldsmiths College, August 1975," Olaseinde remembers. "That would be our last gig together."

Gaffney, who attended the ill-fated Goldsmiths date, remembers a tense scene: The audience ("made up of mostly design students," Gaffney snorts) appeared indifferent to the group's African-oriented sound, seemingly confirming Ifedioranma's conviction that the "Afro" identification was limiting the group's acceptance by a mainstream audience. Meanwhile, the presence of Gaffney and McLean waiting in the wings fueled the resentment amongst the other members. "The band knew that Larry was going to replace them with me and Greg, both of us with hair down to our waists," Gaffney laughs. "After the gig there was an almighty bust-up! Marshall amps were flying through the air and people were getting generally rather upset."

"We were carrying out the equipment after the gig," Olaseinde says. "Everybody was arguing. And when one of the expensive Marshalls was smashed, that made it worse and it turned into a big fight! After that, we went our separate ways." OFO the Black Company—the audacious ensemble of Nigerian musicians who just three short years earlier had blazed the way forward for Afro Rock—was officially dead. However, OFO—the multiracial, weirdy-beardy, prog-jam band—kept on rocking. "I always found that Larry had just about the thickest skin a musician could possess," said Gaffney. "Nothing would get to him."

With the addition of a second guitarist, Rob Pinnock, the group started gigging around the city, drawing enthusiastic crowds with their fusion of Afro, reggae, and post-*Bitches Brew* jazz-rock. OFO's new direction finally reignited Decca's interest and the group was rushed into the studio to record a new album with producer Eddy Grant - himself well-versed in packaging rock fusion for the British public with his own band, the Equals. "Larry wanted to re-do all the old Black Company songs in a more European way," Gaffney recalled. "We did a new version of 'Allah Wakbarr' titled 'A-Ya-Ya," and 'Let's Go' and other songs." Also recorded was a tune that had become a staple of their live repertoire, a floor-shaking rock stomper called "We Will Rock You" which Gaffney maintained until his death in 2011 was appropriated by the flamboyant British rock band Queen for their 1977 arena anthem of the same name. Decca, however, was less than impressed with the results, deemed the album still "too ethnic," and promptly shelved it.

After Decca's final rejection, disillusion again set in; Keith and McLean left, and eventually Gaffney drifted away to join Eric Burdon. Undeterred, Ifedioranma assembled yet another OFO lineup and took them to Nigeria for FESTAC '77 - the 2nd World African Festival of Arts and Culture - held in Lagos that summer. But what was meant to be a triumphant homecoming turned into Ifedioranma's Waterloo as tragedy struck: one of the

ABOVE: IGBO TRAINEES, BIAFRA. 1968. FOLLOWING SPREAD: MEMBERS OF THE FUNKEES AND THE STRANGERS HANGING OUT WITH FANS IN OWERRI. (STANDING, LEFT TO RIGHT) UNIDENTIFIED, ANII HOFNAR (STRANGERS), UNIDENTIFIED, GAB ZANI (STRANGERS), BOB MIGA (STRANGERS), UNIDENTIFIED, OKEREKE (FUNKEES), SAM MCKING (STRANGERS). (SQUATTING, LEFT TO RIGHT): DANNY HEIBS

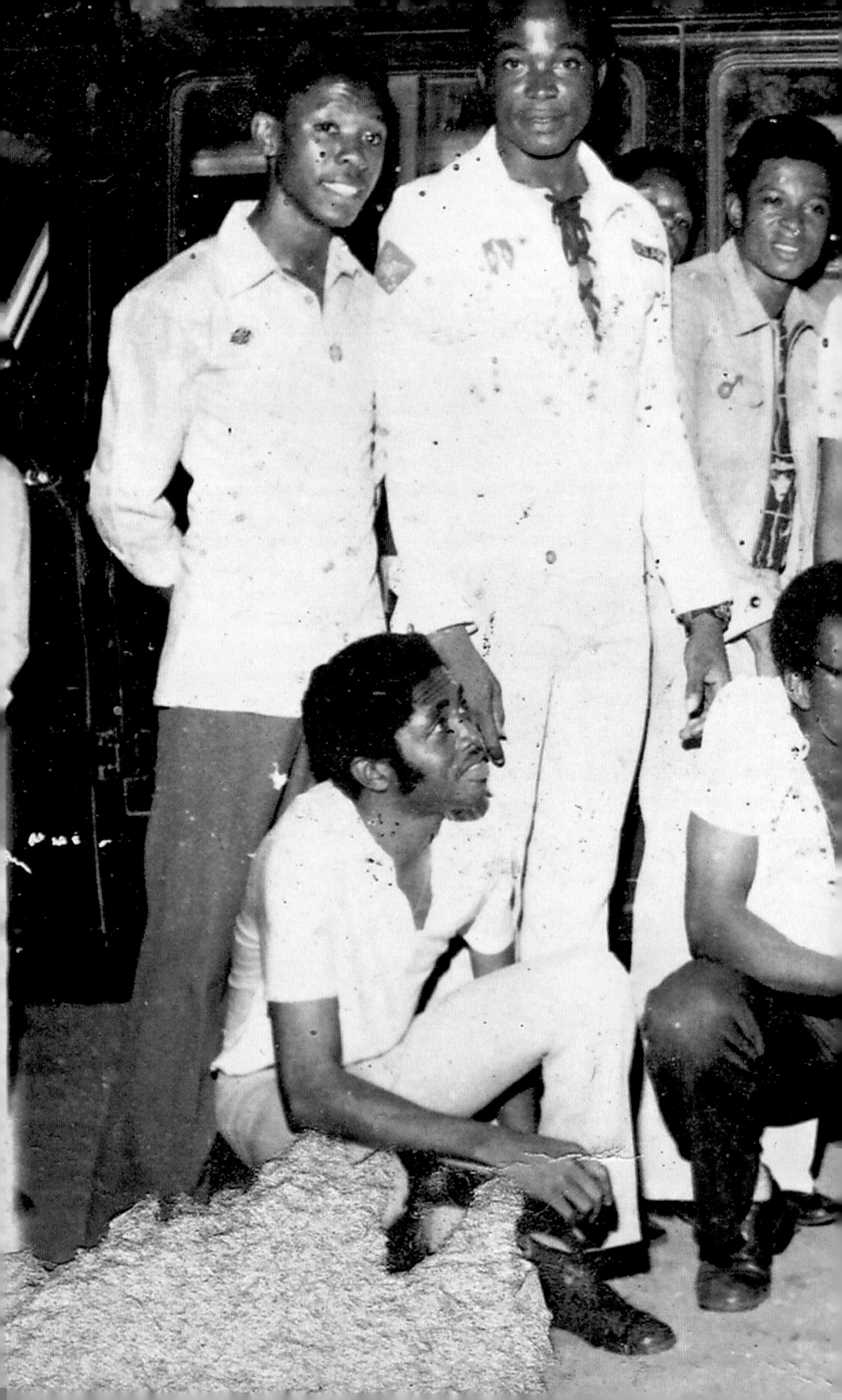

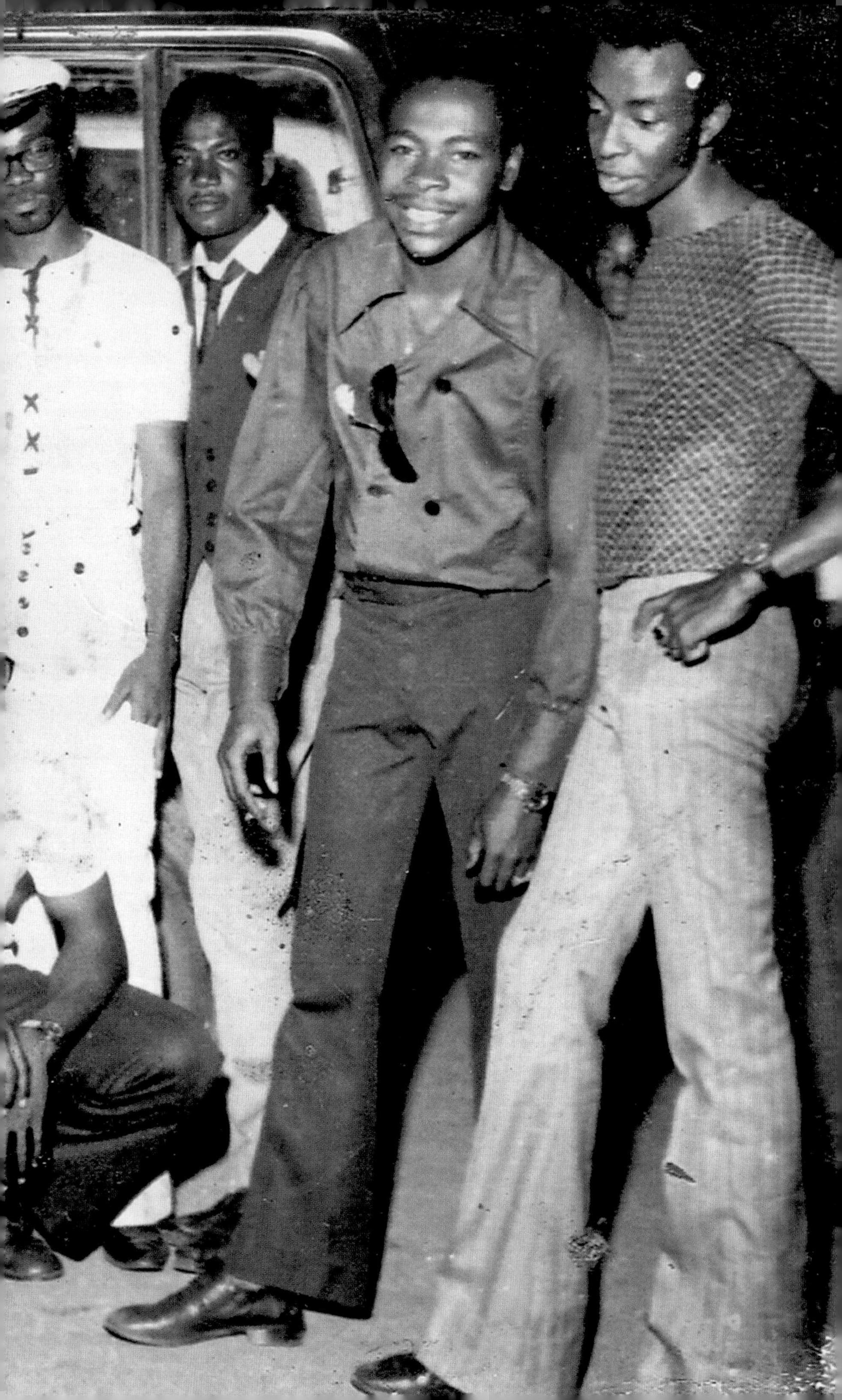

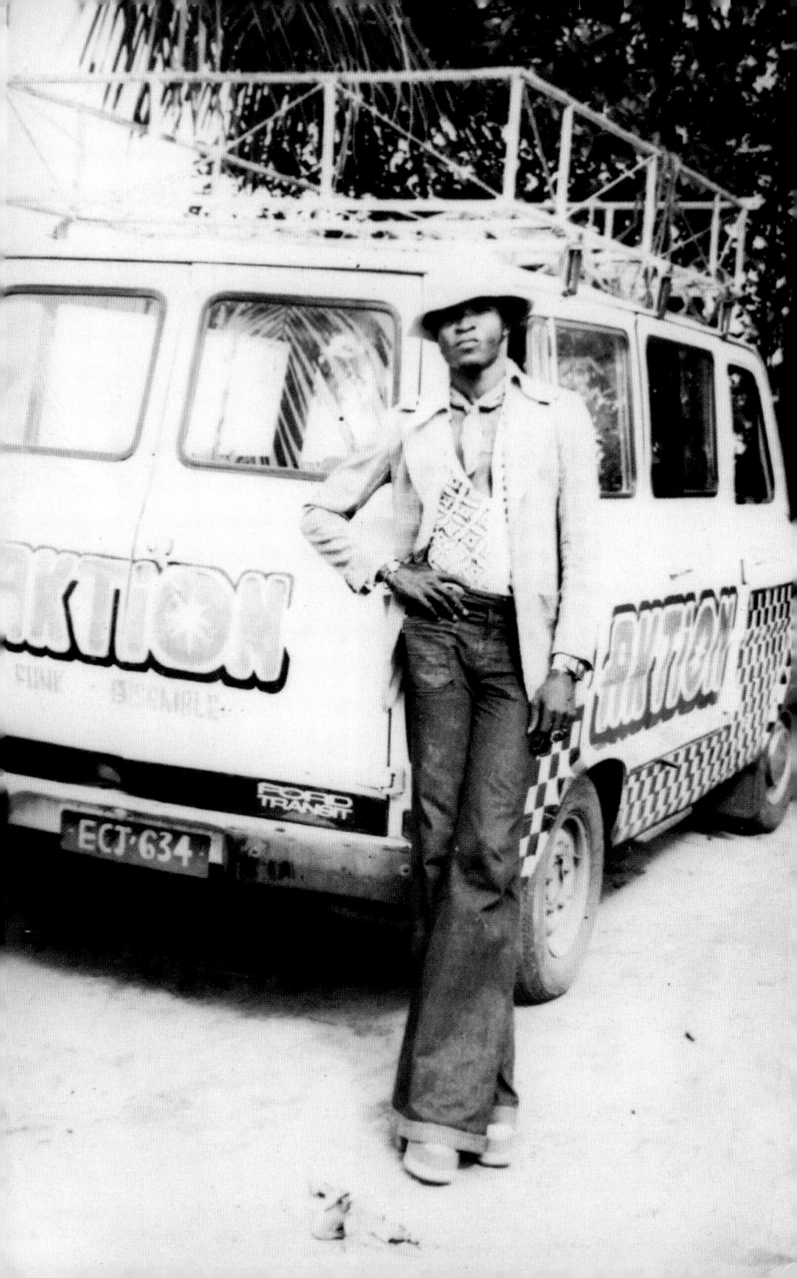
FORD
TRANSIT
ECJ·634

band members drowned while swimming in a river and Ifedioranma found himself in a dispute with bandleader Aigbe Lebarty which ended with Lebarty forcefully seizing all of Ifedioranma's gear, thus spelling OFO's demise.

The ever-tenacious Ifedioranma, however, refused to relinquish his vision and denied all rumors of OFO's demise. Settling back in Nigeria, he released *Fonkafrika*, a dubiously contrived "live" album cobbled together from concert fragments recorded during the latter-prog era and heavily overdubbed with new studio performances. The album attracted little notice. Ifedioranma still commanded a degree of respect among those old enough to remember the force with which OFO the Black Company had blown the doors off the Nigerian music industry a decade earlier, but by and large it was clear the business had moved on without him. Scoring a production deal for a while with the rising independent Tabansi label, Ifedioranma continued to work with other artists while he talked up his big plans to resurrect OFO, but it never came to pass. Larry Ifedioranma Jr. and OFO the Black Company were mostly an obscure memory when he died in 2005.

After Ifedioranma's passing, Gaffney reminisced fondly on his time with OFO: "I've been around a long time now, and I have never heard anything since which comes anywhere near to what we did then. For two years we lived together in each other's pockets, playing every day, sometimes all day… Larry was a very happy man and his composing was prodigious. He was fifteen years ahead of his time. I learned a lot from him, and I miss him very much. His catchphrase was 'Music makes me happy.'"

PART THREE

RETURN TO A NEW NORMAL IN EASTERN NIGERIA

A CALL TO AKTION

The war may have riven the soul of the country, but the true depth of its tragedy—its cost in civilian lives and property—was not fully recognized by the majority of Nigerians until years after it had ended. During the course of the war itself, the theater of combat was largely contained to the Eastern region and behind a firewall of government propaganda that denied the country was at war at all—it was just a "police action" to take care of that "small matter" of a "few motley rebels" who would shortly be "dispatched." So from 1967 to 1970, life carried on as normal for citizens of the Western and Northern regions, with many virtually unaware that while they did the Mashed Potato and the Boogaloo at soul music extravaganzas, federal Nigerian troops were massacring millions of their countrymen or enforcing sanctions that lead to rampant starvation on the other side of the country.

Not that they weren't doing the Mashed Potato and the Boogaloo in the East too; while the predominant image of Civil War-era Biafra is that of skeletal infants crawling through dirt roads littered with wreckage and corpses, for the duration of the war there was an uplifting music scene that moved from town to town ahead of the incoming federal forces.

"Music was very important during the war," says Renny Pearl, bass player in the wartime pop band the Figures. "You have to understand that most people had lost everything. Their entire lives were shattered. Music was the only thing keeping everybody's spirits up. So during the war, it was not strange to see that, when word goes out that we're playing a concert, people will trek on foot from miles away to come and see us. And this is not just free shows, you know! People were paying to buy tickets, so popular groups like the Hykkers and the Fractions made a lot of money during the war."

The Biafran military administration was quick to recognize the morale-boosting benefits (as well as the financial rewards) of having rock groups in their fulltime employ and summarily began to conscript popular bands like the Wings, the In-Crowd and the Admirals. The importance of the rock bands was not lost on the conquering Nigerian Army after the surrender of Biafra in January 1970. Both as a means of entertaining its triumphant soldiers and pacifying the devastated local populace, the 3rd Marine Commando division decreed that all of its outposts across Eastern Nigeria would have an in-house rock band.

BIAFRAN COMBAT VOLUNTEERS IN FORMATION. 1968.

"The army helped them so much in the East," reflects Micro Mike. "Because of the army, they had support while we in Lagos were struggling. We were just kids, we didn't have money to buy good instruments. Many of us were still playing with borrowed or rented instruments. And it was hard for us to get booked in venues because the clubs didn't take us seriously as professional musicians. But in the East, the army gave them instruments, gave them a place to play every night, gave them an audience. I think that is why the rock groups in the East lasted longer while in Lagos the movement died out quicker. It was hard for us to sustain ourselves in Lagos."

It's probably unfair to completely credit the military's subsidies for the endurance of the Eastern rock scene. While the army did provide the initial impetus, most of the groups soon struck out on their own and continued to enjoy enthusiastic support from audiences across Eastern Nigeria throughout the 1970s. A more nuanced evaluation of the situation might take into account a deeper emotional connection to the music bonded in the traumatic experience of the war. In Lagos, soul and rock were little more than a fad, a passing fever. For the people in the East, it was rock music that got them through Hell.

The Aktion Funk Ensemble was the next phase in the evolution of the Actions, the first of the postwar army groups. The Actions themselves had come together out of the remnants of a Biafran military group, the Figures. "The Figures were the second major pop group in Eastern Nigeria, after the Postmen," says founder Renny Pearl. "We came together in Port Harcourt around 1966, before the war. This was when we had all just left school."

The original Figures featured Pearl on bass, Lemmy Faith and Timmy Show on guitars and Berkley Jones (later of BLO) on drums. The group swiftly amassed a rabid following even as the war erupted in July 1967, but when Port Harcourt was captured by federal forces in 1968 they were forced underground, trekking from place to place, performing in makeshift hospitals and refugee camps in remote villages. It was during this chaotic period that Show was separated from the group (eventually resurfacing in the In-Crowd) and Jones stepped up to take over on guitar. To fill Jones' vacated drum stool, the group picked up a local youth named Chyke Madu.

"I had just learned to play the drums so I only knew one beat," Madu remembers. "Actually, I wasn't even playing drums at the time. I had learned how to play 'Cold Sweat' by James Brown on the tabletop. But when the Figures came and played in my village, I was interested in joining them. So I showed them I could play 'Cold Sweat' and they took me in! Berkley Jones taught me a lot; I think he really wanted to find a new drummer to replace him because he was eager to pick up the guitar."

Along the way, the group also added organist Pat Moore before being drafted by the Biafran Navy, outfitted in white, bellbottomed naval rigs and rechristened the Sailors (a name they resented and mostly ignored). By the end of 1969, with Biafra rapidly losing ground and naval ports blocked off, the Navy unit fell into stasis, and the Sailors sunk with it.

"We had nothing to do since most of the base was deserted," says Pearl. "The group quietly fell apart as we found different activities to fill our time. Lemmy went into business smuggling goods from Nigeria to Biafra. Pat went back to his hometown of Nkwerre. And then he came back some days later to tell us that there was a new group trying to start up there, so we should all go and join. I was already sitting in with an air force band called the Air Raid so I didn't go, but Chyke and Berkley went back with him to join that group, which of course turned out to be the Funkees."

Pearl continues, "By the time the war ended, we didn't even know it. We were on that deserted base, just us and some other civilians hanging around. All the military personnel were gone. We hadn't heard any bombs or gunfire for days, and there were rumors that the war was over. After some days, I decided I would find out for myself. So I dressed up in my white sailor uniform, slung my acoustic guitar over my shoulder and started walking up the road. I said I would not stop until I saw someone."

Pearl had only gotten a few miles before he found himself ambushed by the advancing 13th Brigade of the 3rd Marine Commando, who believed he was a fleeing combatant. "They had all these guns pointed directly on me!" Pearl now laughs. "I showed them my guitar and told them 'I'm not a soldier, I'm a musician.' They asked me where I'm coming from, I told them I'm coming from the base. So they asked me if soldiers were hiding there. I told them all the soldiers are gone. It's just me, my band and some other civilians. They said, 'Okay... Let's go back to the base. But if we get there and we see any soldiers, it's you that we're shooting first.'"

Once the 13th Brigade found the base indeed devoid of military personnel, they demanded Pearl prove he was truly a noncombatant musician by putting on a show. "Remember now, my band was gone by this time," Pearl says. "It was just me and Lemmy still there. But I was able to round up a few guys from Air Raid and we played. The soldiers danced and enjoyed themselves, you know, with some of the women who were around. At the end of it, they told us, 'Okay, you're coming with us.'"

The Brigade commander dubbed the new group "the Actions" and put them on salary as the official band of the 13th Brigade. As the Brigade became famous for its "Action 13" band, other brigades rushed to secure their own groups. The Actions' popularity spread as they became the first Eastern rock band to travel to Lagos to record a single at EMI Studios and perform at Fela Ransome-Kuti's Afrika Shrine. But by 1974, the group wanted out.

"The main problem was the fact that the brigade commander had decided that all of us must enlist in the army," Pearl says. "We were employed by the army as contracted performers, but we were not soldiers. They wanted to conscript us into the army as individuals. We didn't want that."

"And then we had been performing with the army, selling out shows. We had made several records. And because we were owned by the army, all the money we made went to them while they paid us a meager salary. Other army groups that came after us had already broken away from the army and were controlling their own careers. We wanted more control, but if we allowed ourselves to be conscripted, we would have even less! So we had to get away from the army."

One small problem: the 13th Brigade owned the names "the Actions" and "Action 13," as well as all the group's instruments, leaving them with no choice but to dissolve

IGBO SOLDIERS, BIAFRA. 1968.

"IN THE JUNGLE" BY THE HYGRADES, RELEASED IN 1972.

the group altogether. With the Actions dead, Pearl moved to Lagos alone to try to start a new band, but after a few false starts he received a message from a young entrepreneur named Ben Okonkwo back in the Eastern city of Aba: "He told me to come to Aba immediately because he wanted to sponsor the Actions, to give us new instruments, a bus, everything."

Okonkwo had recently struck gold on his BEN label with singles by the Eastern rock groups the Apostles, Heralds 7, One World and the Doves, and he intended to launch a new label, Clover Records, dedicated to showcasing the new cutting-edge rock of the East in the LP format. And he wanted Action 13 to serve as the cornerstone of the new imprint.

Pearl rushed back to the East and put together a new, heavier lineup of Action 13, now known as the Aktion Funk Ensemble, or just Aktion.

Aktion's 1975 debut album *Groove the Funk* barely registered a blip on the Lagos radar but sold hundreds of thousands of copies in the Eastern and Northern parts of the country, establishing Aktion as a top-grossing touring attraction. The group's second album, *Celebration* (1977) arrived as Aktion settled in to a plush gig as resident band at Zeina Niteclub in the city of Warri, renowned for its colorful and competitive nightlife circuit. However, management and financial troubles gradually ate away at the fabric of the group, leading to Pearl's decision to officially end Aktion in 1979.

OPENING ENUGU: RISE OF THE HYGRADES

For the people of Eastern Nigeria, the erstwhile denizens of the short-lived Republic of Biafra, one of the clearest symbols of the return of some kind of normalcy after the war was the resurgence of Enugu. Enugu had been the political, commercial and intellectual capital of the Eastern Region before the war. After the secession, Enugu was elevated to the national capital of Biafra. As such, it was a natural target for the federal forces and became one of the first cities in Biafra to be taken down, leading to a frantic mass flight. Once Biafra tendered its surrender, the federal administration committed to restoring the heart of the East to life, and issued the call for all displaced Enugu residents to return to the deserted city.

"The government had told everybody it was safe to come back to Enugu, but people were afraid," says Chyke Madu, by then a member of the Funkees. "There was a rumor going around that it was a trap, that once they got everybody back into the city, they were going to murder everybody. Believe it or not, it was the music that made people feel safe." Madu claims that the Funkees' music let Enugu's residents know that "normal life had returned" as well.

The Funkees' success in "opening" Enugu spurred other groups in the region to move to the city, and in no time, the Enugu axis became home to a lively soul and rock music scene with bands such as the Wings, the Soulmen, the Heroes, the Road Runners, Salt & Pepper Organization and a score of others. One of the most revered – and mysterious—was Goddy Oku's Hygrades.

Oku had been one of the pioneers of the Enugu rock scene, first gaining notice in the 1960s as the lead guitarist of the Postmen. What made Oku a local legend, though, was his skill as an engineer. The son of an electrician, Oku started tinkering with circuits from childhood and by his teens he was constructing speaker systems and amplifiers for cash-strapped musicians, as well as building guitars and drum kits.

During the war, Oku led an army-sponsored soul group called the Silhouettes, which also featured his teenage protégé Justus "Jay U" Nnakwe. After the war, Oku and Nnakwe returned to Enugu and thought about forming a new band, but first had to pick up the pieces of their lives – literally. "I can remember when we got to Goddy's house," says Nnakwe. "All down the road, you would see houses with the roofs blown off them. The street was just filled with household items all over the place. Myself, I had to go and look for my family because they had fled the city when Enugu was captured. And I had to think about getting back to school, too."

While Nnakwe was at school, Oku took a gig playing lead guitar for the highlife star Celestine Ukwu, where he remained for a year. In 1971, Oku left Ukwu to get back to his roots in rock n' roll, with a new group he called the

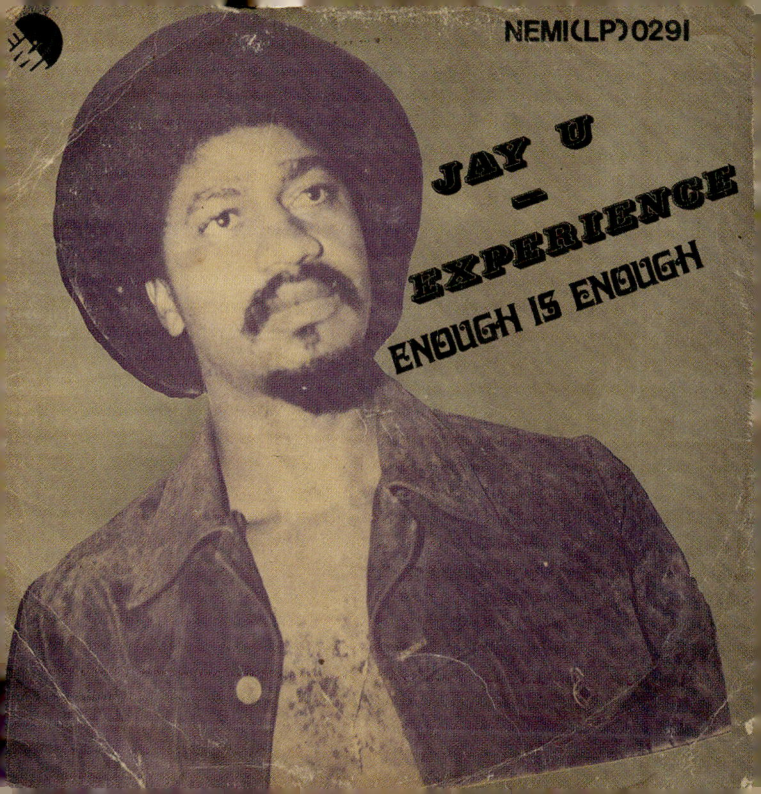
NEMI(LP)0291
JAY U
–
EXPERIENCE
ENOUGH IS ENOUGH

"KEEP ON MOVING" BY THE HYGRADES, RELEASED IN 1971.

Hygrades. They were a loose aggregation whose lineup revolved around Oku and whose sound epitomized the dirty rhythm & blues style of Enugu soul. Before other groups from the region had started recording or appearing on the radio, the Hygrades ruled Enugu's limited airwaves (thanks, that is, to Oku's homemade radio transmitter – which he used to broadcast the band's rehearsal sessions).

When EMI began to aggressively scout talent in the East, the Hygrades were among the first to release a record, scoring regional hits with the singles "Baby" b/w "Jumping Cat" and "Keep On Moving" b/w "Rough Rider" in 1971. Two more singles, "In The Jungle" b/w "In The Jungle (Instrumental)" and "Somebody's Gonna Lose or Win" b/w "Day Dreamer" followed in 1972. Just as the Hygrades prepared to expand their base with a tour, Oku underwent a religious epiphany, distancing himself from secular music but giving the blessing to guitarist Nnakwe and bassist Chuba "Drago" Uboma to continue the group without him.

The Oku-less Hygrades were a taste that some of the audience was not ready to swallow. "I was into heavy metal," says Nnakwe. "Deep Purple, Led Zeppelin, Black Sabbath. By the time I came back to the Hygrades... I was moving us more in that acid rock direction. But the vibes of the time were already changing towards a more pop sound, thanks to the popularity of groups like the Apostles and the Wings. So when we would come on the stage after them and play our heavy metal, people thought we were playing noise."

With the new Hygrades coming off as too extreme for the scene, the group disbanded. Drago and Nnakwe formed a new, more mainstream outfit called Speed Limit, achieving a local hit on EMI with "Hosanna" b/w "You Got Me Down" and drummer Innocent "Stoneface" Iwuagwu went off to lead Life Everlasting, releasing a series of EMI singles, including "Love is Free" b/w "Agawalam Mba." But when the young players of Life Everlasting deserted him to form the commercial pop group, Sweet Breeze, Stoneface returned to his former Hygrades compatriots. They still burned with the desire to play heavier music even as the climate shifted towards lighter fare, and the result was the People Rock Outfit, or P.R.O. The group started off on a high note, powered by the prestige of the Hygrades' legacy, snagging the plum spot opening for Jimmy Cliff during the reggae superstar's visit to Enugu in 1975. P.R.O.'s self-titled 1976 album was a virtual Hygrades reunion, with Nnakwe, Iwuagwu and Drago's rhythm section, and Oku on keyboards and production.

P.R.O. continued to play in and around Enugu, watching as the Eastern music scene slowly went commercial. Not surprisingly, the P.R.O. LP didn't make any significant waves, but they were intent on trying to make another record to revive the Enugu hard rock scene. Nnakwe's "solo" record as Jay U Experience, *Enough is Enough*, released in 1978, was an attempt to compromise, to offer a heavy sound that was lighter on the sonic abrasiveness that had sheared off much of the Hygrades' audience. As Drago wrote in the album's sleeve notes:

> *This album speaks volumes for itself and imparts to the cultured musik enthusiast the grounding in rudiments of musik which ensures the marked absence of discords and other musical taboos that have been so recklessly broken by all but a few in the musik scene of this land. This brilliant work is - make no mistakes about this - a privileged escursion [sic] into a world of non-discordant rock.*

Despite all efforts, the album failed to reverse the trend of the times. P.R.O.'s brand of hard rock was officially passé, and the group quietly split up as its members pursued careers in other industries.

THE APOSTLES' FUZZ-FUNK SERMONS

The Apostles of Aba were one of the most consistently popular (and amongst purists, one of the most controversial) groups of the Eastern rock circuit. Their rise served to greatly expand the market for rock but caused the hardcore fans to worry that the scene had become too mainstream and ripe for opportunists. The beef with the Apostles was that they were faking the funk, so to speak. The group had existed since the early 1970s, originally as a highlife ag-

ABOVE: DRAGO UBOMA FROM P.R.O. 1976. FOLLOWING SPREAD: THE APOSTLES OF ABA (LEFT TO RIGHT) CHYKE FUSSION, HARRISON MBA, BENJAMIN DAVIDSON, CHICAGO WOHA, JOEL MADUBUIKE, HENRY ASU TANDU, WALTON ARUNGWA. MID 1970S.

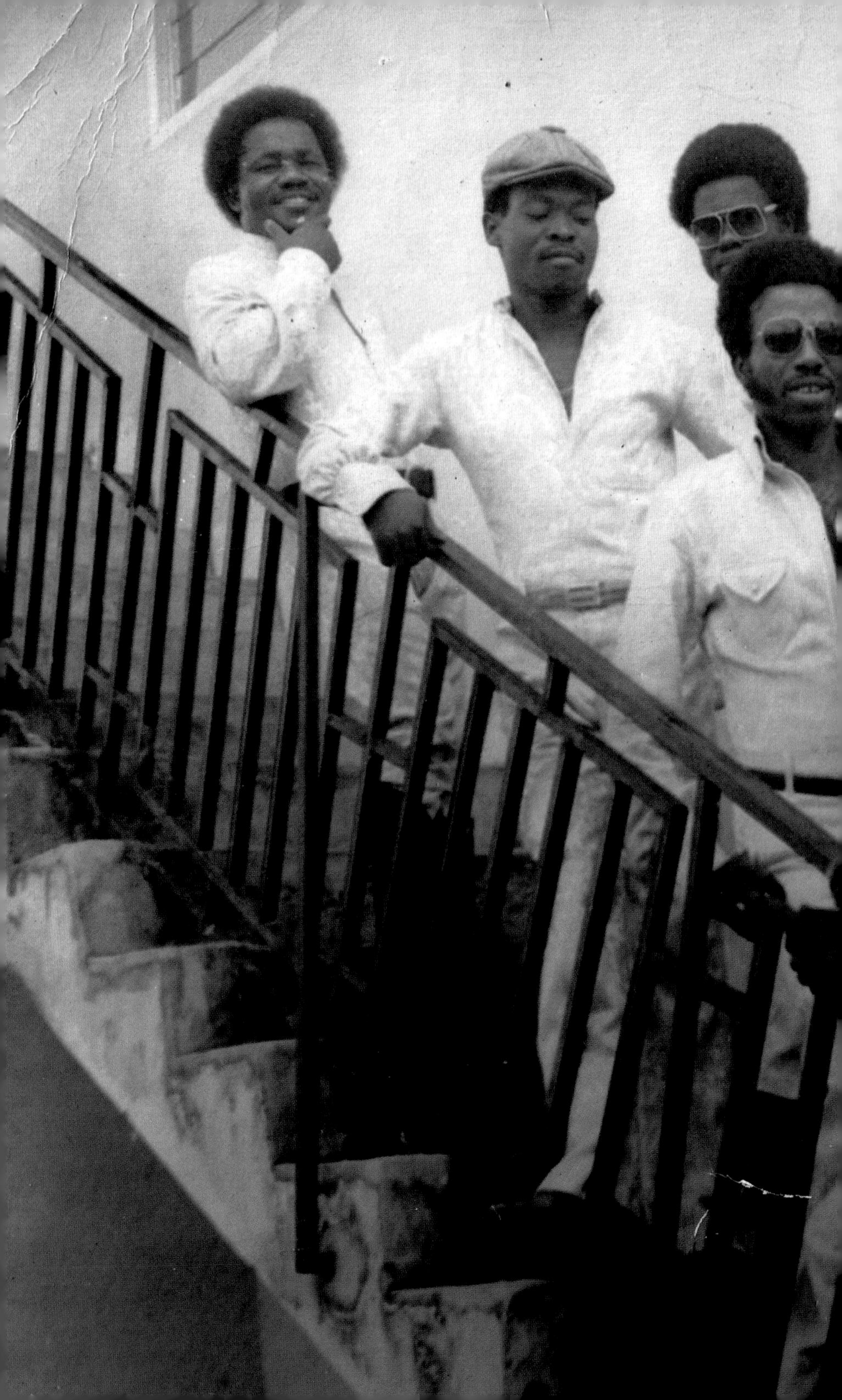

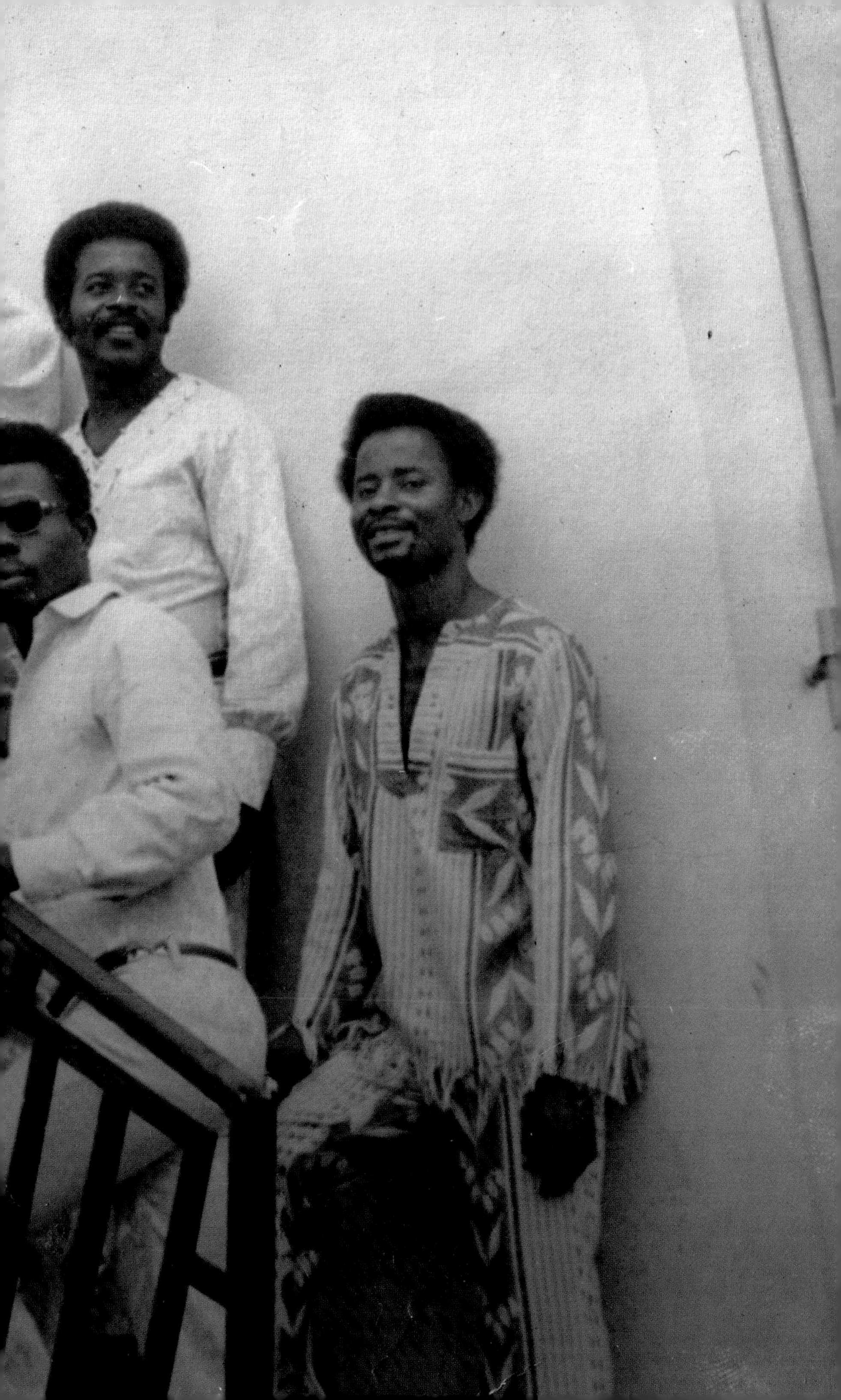

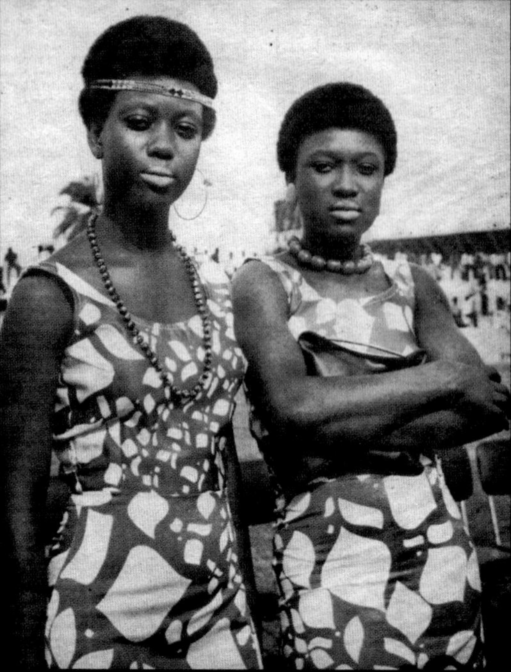

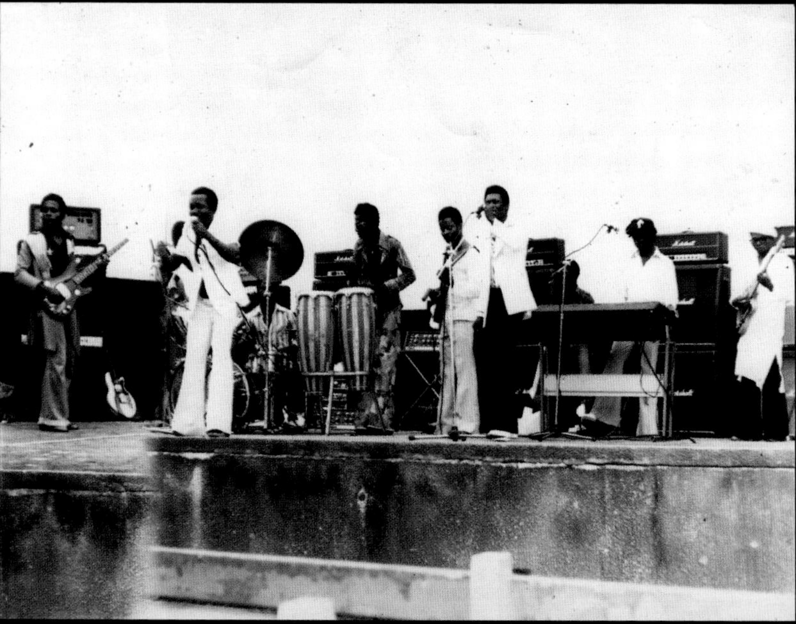

gregation called Prince Walton Arungwa & His Super 7, and even recorded a few singles for Philips. Arungwa was a street hustler who started playing guitar in the late 1960s in the belief that music was the next big game and a good way to avoid being drafted, so his authenticity as a musician was constantly questioned. As nightlife in Aba began to resurge after the war, Arungwa shifted his band's direction towards Congo guitar music, recognizing that this was the preferred soundtrack of women of the *demimonde*.

But soul music was the music of the beautiful people (and the people who wanted to know beautiful people) so he knew he had to integrate some soul numbers into his repertoire. For this purpose, he hired a young James Brown enthusiast named Chyke Fussion, who had seen combat as a teen during the war. The addition of keyboardist Louis Goldfinger, whose sinuous organ leads made up for Arungwa's less than adequate guitar playing, modernized the Super 7's (now renamed the City Stars) sound. When Aba's leading group the Funkees announced that they were abandoning their lucrative contract with the 12th Brigade, competition flared up amongst all the bands in town in the hopes of taking over the contract. Arungwa put in a bid by transforming the City Stars into the Apostles Rock Group. The contract ultimately went to the Wings, but the Apostles won the attention of Ben Okonkwo, then preparing to launch his BEN label. The Apostles were the first group on the label and their first two singles were hits, big enough to tempt EMI into offering them a contract.

More hit singles followed at EMI, and after a membership shakeup that included the departure of Goldfinger, in 1976 the group released its first, self-titled album, sometimes referred to by the title of its first track "Never Too Late," which opens with a fiery guitar solo played by Arungwa. Or was it? "I don't think he played that," Fussion says. "Walton was not really a rock guitarist, and many times we had to bring in Felix Odey to play his parts."

"I don't know if I played it," says Felix "Feladey" Odey, who subbed and ghosted with a wide range of groups as a guitar for hire in the 1970s. "I might have played it, I'm not sure. I played on a lot of records in those days so I can't remember. I know that at times I had to come in to coach Walton, to teach him solos and all that. He just didn't have that blues in his soul."

Regardless of the debate over their authenticity, the Apostles remained a broad favorite group throughout the 1970s, freely switching lanes from rock to funk to pop to reggae to disco and boogie before finally hanging it up in 1984. "To be a successful band, you have to be able to play any kind of music," says Chyke Fussion. "No matter what kind of crowd you find yourself in front of, you should be able to play something they will enjoy. I don't think that is a bad thing. That is what makes a band last."

FINDING THE FOUNDERS 15

Like Action 13, Founders 15 was a group that remained closely associated with the army in the public imagination (in particular with the 15th Brigade of Port Harcourt) though it actually reached its height of success independent from military benefaction. The original members of the Founders came together in 1971 as young, aspiring musicians recruited by singer-guitarist Lasbrey Ojukwu (late of the In-Crowd) to form a new band called the Semi-Colon. The original Semi-Colon consisted of Ojukwu on lead guitar, Kenneth "Nek" Adirika on rhythm, Sunday Sloppy on bass, Uzzi Kriis on drums and a former Biafran Army captain named Iyke Peters on lead vocals.

When Peters got wind of the news that the 28th Brigade in the town of Obosi had purchased a new set of instruments and was looking for a band to play them, the entire Semi-Colon lineup left Ojukwu and moved to Obosi to become Rock 2-8 (with the addition of organist Kevin Coburn from the Hygrades). A short while later, the dissolution of the 28th Brigade saw the group reassigned to the 15th Brigade and renamed the Founders. As the top band in Port Harcourt, one of the biggest urban centers of the East, the Founders became a main attraction. Soon enough though, the band was faced with the conscription issue as the army commanded its members to become uniformed, enlisted men. Kriis, Sloppy and Coburn conceded, welcoming the career stability of military life, but Peters and Adirika resisted. Uzzi, Coburn and Sloppy were reassigned to another band in Northern Nigeria while Peters was allowed to

"I CANT BE SATISFIED" BY THE FOUNDERS 15, RELEASED IN 1974.

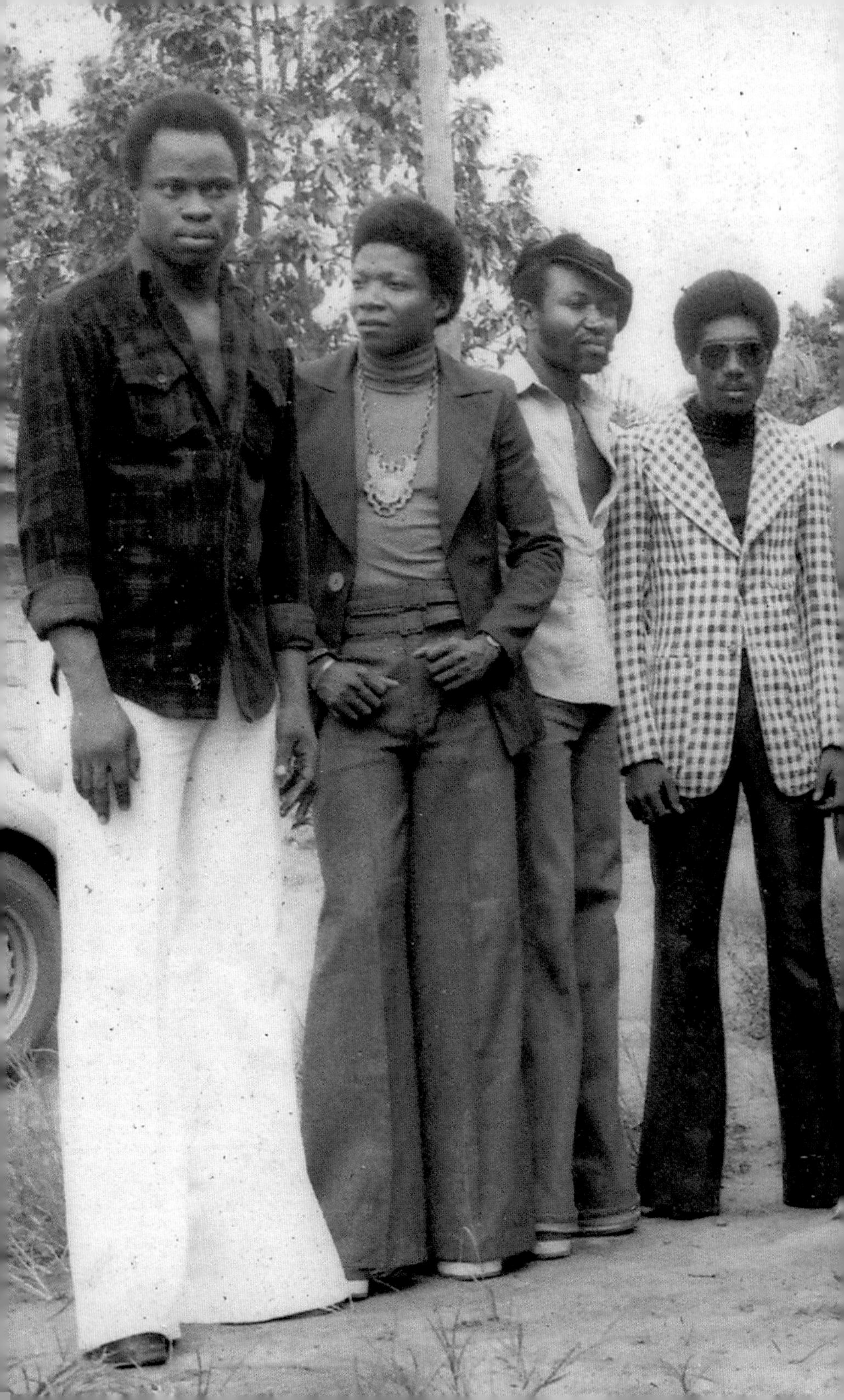

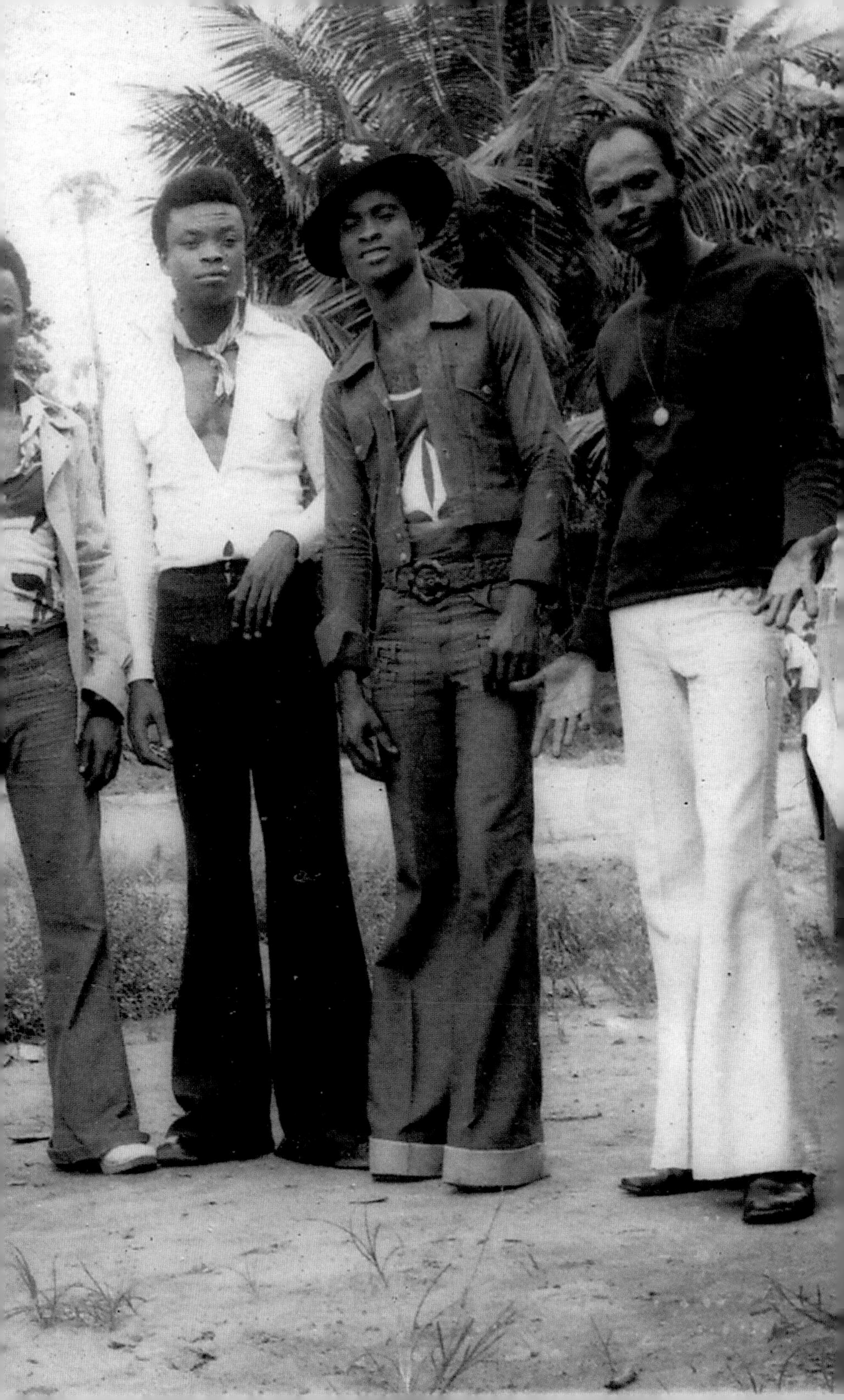

ABOVE: FOUNDERS 15 ON NTA 6 ABA'S NOW SOUND! TV PROGRAM. MID 1970S.
BELOW: THE SEMI-COLON OUTSIDE EMI STUDIOS, LAGOS. CIRCA 1977. PREVIOUS SPREAD: FOUNDERS 15 (LEFT TO RIGHT) SONY ENANG, MARSHALL UDO, IYKE PETERS, SAM AKPATI, NEK ADIRIKA AND UNIDENTIFIED TOURING HORN AND PERCUSSION PLAYERS. MID 1970S.

continue the Founders in Port Harcourt. To replenish the group's membership, he went to Aba to recruit musicians and was instantly dazzled by bass player Marshall Udo.

Like Peters, Udo was an alumnus of Semi-Colon's school, though he had come from a later class. (Ojukwu had gone through three iterations of the band in two years as his players continually defected.) Udo's funky bass, flamboyant attire and flashy stage presence had brought a new youthful energy to Semi-Colon but he elected to leave the group in order to resume his education, which had been interrupted by the war.

"I had to leave Semi-Colon because I promised my parents I would go back to school, but somehow that didn't happen," Udo explains. "Instead, I found myself playing with the Funkees in Aba." The Funkees had recently been invited to London and were trying to revamp their membership before the trip. Udo had been invited to try out for the group, to the consternation of its current bassist Danny Heibs. "I could tell Danny was not happy to see me around. There was a negative feeling when I was there, so I removed myself from that environment."

Udo joined the NoNo, a group composed chiefly of disgruntled players from the Funkees circle, led by ex-Funkees guitarist Tex Soul. There was a lot of action surrounding ex-Funkees members on the eve of the band's trip to the UK. Lead singer Mohammed Ahidjo had reputedly written the Funkees' biggest hits only to be informed that he would not be accompanying the group to London. Guitarist Feladey had been recruited to replace Tex Soul in the London edition of the Funkees but bowed out in the face of hostility from guitarist Harry Mosco, who felt upstaged by his theatrical showmanship. NoNo's lineup was rounded out by keyboardist Sony Enang and drummer Ifeanyi Akpati.

The NoNo had managed to record a single for Polydor but the group was already splintering due to creative differences between Tex Soul and Ahidjo. Eventually, Ahidjo was re-absorbed into the Funkees when the London promoter declared that the deal was off if they didn't come with the guy who'd actually sang on the records. With the NoNo seemingly adrift, Udo, Enang and

Akpati felt they might be better off following Peters to the Founders.

Udo's arrival added a funky and psychedelic vibe to the Founders, especially when he began to introduce material he had workshopped during his time with the Funkees and the NoNo. "Ahidjo and myself were quite close," Udo says. "We used to write songs together, and when he went back to the Funkees he took some of the ideas we had developed together. When I listen to that first Funkees album that they recorded in London, I can hear my own feelings on it. Like the song on that album, 'I Can't Be Satisfied,' we wrote that together when we were feeling frustrated with all the problems in the NoNo."

He closes: "The version by the Funkees is closer to the original version we wrote. You can even hear it when he sings 'I can't be satisfied, no, no.' It was originally 'I can't be satisfied—NoNo!"... and then the NoNo will sing back to him, 'I can't be satisfied!' I also ended up making my own version of the song with Founders but I changed it around a little. Founders' version has a different melody and the words say 'I can't be satisfied *no more*.'"

PART FOUR

SCHOOLBOY ROCK

THE NEW BREED ARRIVES:
PROTO-METAL AND FUZZ-TINGED POP

"One of the problems with our rock scene in the 1970s, why it couldn't really sustain itself for long, is that it was, in a way, elitist." Dele Olaseinde declares. "Our audience was relatively small, compared to the people who were listening to maybe King Sunny Ade or Ebenezer Obey. They were able to reach the man in the street, the uneducated working-class people, while we were appealing mainly to a comparatively small group of students and other hip young adults."

He continues: "Even Fela, with his early Afro Beat records, his audience was this same hip elite. But he soon figured out how to appeal to the working class and restyle himself as the Hero of the People. That

ZEROLAS BATTERIES COMPANY LTD.
LICENSED BY THE BOARD OF CUSTOMS
AND EXCISE
AS MOTOR VEHICLE BATTERIES
MANUFACTURERS.
"EXCISE FACTORY No. 526"

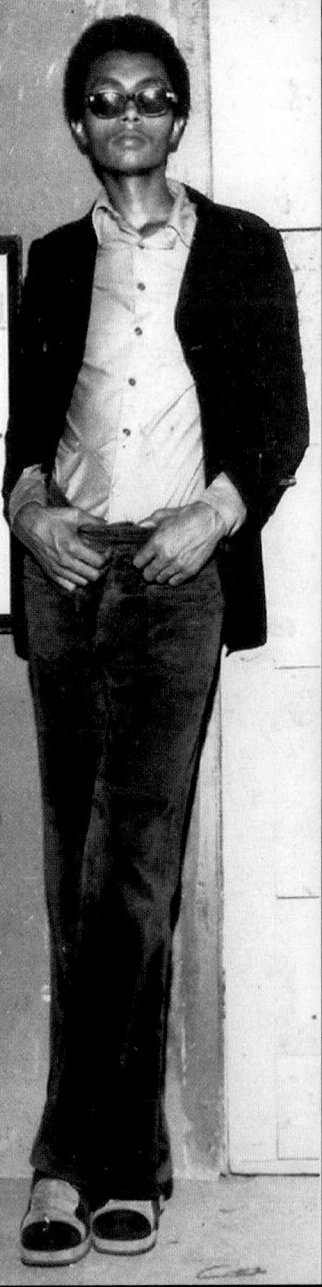

SOGA BENSON (GUITAR) AND DAPO OLUMIDE (KEYBOARDS) AT OFEGE'S FINAL LIVE PERFORMANCE, LAGOS. 1977

GROTTO ON STAGE IN LAGOS. (LEFT TO RIGHT) SOGA BENSON, MARTIN AMENACHI, SKIDD IKEMEFUNA, 1976

"GRACEFUL BIRD" BY WAR-HEAD CONSTRICTION, RELEASED IN 1973.

was one of the reasons he was able to stay around much longer than the rock groups."

But if rock music in general was perceived as a somewhat specialized taste, even more esoteric was the niche-within-a-niche represented by the extra-edgy, post-OFO subgenre that embraced abstraction as poetry, noise as texture, and volume as a virtue. This was music for an audience that was just as likely to freak-out as to get-down, who were enlightened enough to view music as more than just stimulus for dancing or a soundtrack for good times, but as a portal to mind expansion. It was music designed for students—and, in the mid to late 1970s—was increasingly *made* by students.

High school—"secondary school," in local parlance—pop groups had existed in Nigeria since the 1960s, starting with the first acknowledged rock n' roll bands in Nigeria, the Blue Knights and the Strangers. By the early 1970s, a circuit had developed, encompassing the most prestigious secondary schools in Lagos, including the Freemantles from Birch Freeman High School, the Groove Masters from St. Gregory's College, the KC Hotspots of King's College and Igbobi College's IC Rockets. Meanwhile, in the Eastern region of the country, school dances were rocked by the Future Hopes, hailing from Merchants of Light School, Oba, and the Dee-Mites of Dennis Memorial Grammar School, Onitsha.

The "schoolboy rock" phenomenon however finally hit critical mass in 1974 with the arrival of Ofege, a hard-hitting, raw-edged Afro-psych group made up of funky-looking ninth-graders from St. Gregory's. Under the skillful direction of producer Odion Iruoje, Ofege's debut LP *Try and Love* became the biggest-selling album of the Nigerian rock era and kicked off a fad for edgy, psychedelic rock from the campuses of Nigeria's secondary and tertiary education institutions, featuring collegiate psych-rockers such as Tabanaku, Ifa, Sulty & Koku, the New Generation and Stratocaster.

While Ofege might have been the impetus for the flowering of the college rock sub-genre, the inspiration behind Ofege dated back to a few years before *Try and Love*. Ofege was, at its core, a more commercially-angled version of an earlier St. Greg's psych-rock band that went by the formidable name of War-Head Constriction. "War-Head were our seniors in school," Ofege rhythm guitarist and lead singer Melvin Ukachi recalls. "When we were starting out, we looked up to them because they were already kind of established. By the time we were learning how to play our instruments, they had already released a record."

That record was "Graceful Bird" b/w "Shower of Stone," whose dark and menacing proto-metal ambience sounds unlike anything heard on the Nigerian scene before - or after. Released in the summer of 1973, the single was enthusiastically received by the critics, but like most of Afrodisia's post-OFO rock releases, its buzz dissipated before it could make an impact in the broader market. War-Head Constriction continued to do shows (briefly changing their name to V0ID in early 1974), and often paired up with Living Truth, the group formerly known as the Waves. "At this point in Greg's, Ofege was forming and coming up under our wings," War-Head guitarist Martin Amenechi remembers.

THE COLLEGE BAND CIRCUIT:
A LAST STAB AT COMMERCIAL CROSS-OVER

The runaway, broad-based success of Ofege's debut *Try and Love* and their 1976 follow-up *Last of the Origins* proved to be the catalyst that finally thrust underground music into the mainstream, vaulted EMI clean over Afrodisia in the running for the home of heavy rock, and established Odion Iruoje as the man with the magic touch for producing sounds that were progressive yet accessible.

By 1977, with Ofege leaving EMI for Polydor, Iruoje was tasked with finding a new group to replace the label's golden group. Immediately, he began to audition other high school and university bands but found few that struck him as sonically mature. Wilfred Ekanem, who was the bass player and chief creative force in Tirogo, a hard rock aggregation made up of teens from various Lagos high schools, recalls the mad scramble of bands trying to find a home at EMI in the wake of the Ofege phenomenon.

BE NICE TO THE PEOPLE LP BY QUESTION MARK, RELEASED IN 1977.

ABOVE: (LEFT TO RIGHT) PRODUCER ODION IRUOJE, GUITARIST AND SINGER EASY KABAKA BROWN, PRODUCER TONY ESSIEN. MID 1970S. BELOW: EMI ENGINEER EMMAN ODENUSI. MID 1970S.

"EMI was the biggest [label] and the one to be involved with. There was also Decca Records. If you couldn't make EMI, then Decca or Phonogram was your second choice," Ekanem states. "It was very tough getting into EMI. Every time we auditioned it was, 'No, you're not ready, try some other time'" However, Iruoje felt his fortunes had turned around when a young man from Enugu walked into the EMI office and handed him a demo tape bursting with searing guitar rock, confident songwriting and solid pop smarts. Franklin Izuora informed him that the music was entirely conceived and performed by his band Question Mark, composed of students from Dennis Memorial Grammar School and the Merchants of Light School.

"What really impressed Odion," says Question Mark percussionist Uzo Agulefo, "was the fact that Frank had told him that he had played all the instruments. Or he demonstrated that he *could* play all the instruments. Because with Ofege, Odion had had to supplement them in the studio with session musicians." (Every guitar solo on *Try and Love*, for instance, is played by BLO guitarist Berkley Jones.) "I don't think he wanted to position us to compete directly with Ofege or anything, but just to have a different version, or an answer to Ofege from Eastern Nigeria," Agulefo says. "Our sound was very different from what was popular in the East at that time. By the mid 1970s, what was hot in the East was a more pop-soul sound… That was the popular commercial sound. We wanted to take a more adventurous approach, with wild solos, chord inversions, chord solos, all of that!" Iruoje immediately arranged for the group to come to Lagos to start work on an album.

Meanwhile, after auditioning five times, Tirogo finally landed their EMI deal and started work on their debut album, *Float*. With Iruoje's production slate full, the project was assigned to Odion's lieutenant, recording engineer Emmanuel Odenusi, who had started taking baby steps towards the producer's chair. However, Ekanem insists that Odenusi's production credit was largely a formality, and his creative input relatively minimal. "It was customary for the studio manager at the time to stick their name down as the producer since he was tweaking the knobs," Ekanem says, "but I arranged and directed [the record]."

Float followed closely the Ofege style, featuring pop songs set against a backdrop of 6/8 Afro-rhythms and seasoned with generous helpings of Santana-esque guitars, but ultimately lacked the fire and personality that endeared Ofege to the mainstream audience. The album did delight the student crowd, though, and Tirogo remained with EMI for a further two albums that exuded a greater confidence, as the band moved away from their debut's intense psych-rock.

When Question Mark's *Be Nice To The People* was released (also in 1977), it fared no better, landing in the market with a resounding thud. The album attracted a small cult following among university students in the East but failed to register at all in Lagos and other parts of the county. The underperformance of Question Mark, as well as Iruoje's failure to break other school bands such as Tabanaku and Apples, seemed to indicate that Ofege's mainstream moment was a fluke that was not to be replicated: heavy rock was receding once again into the murky depths of the underground from whence it came.

Iruoje maintained faith in Question Mark's promise, but started to rethink the group's approach, considering a smoother, R&B sound. Agulefo recalls Iruoje pitching a new direction for a Question Mark sophomore LP. "He told me he felt bad about how things had gone with the album and he wanted to do another record with us. I remember he gave me this Candi Staton LP and said he wanted us to cover a tune on there."

Indeed, Iruoje's sea change in championing heavy rock was symptomatic of the times, as the style declined in popularity in the wake of disco. War-Head Constriction morphed into Grotto, and after a hard rock-intensive EMI debut sank without a trace, their sophomore effort focused on jazzy disco-funk. Both Ofege and Tirogo pivoted toward more dance-oriented R&B, and then dub and militant rockers-style reggae, which, by the late 1970s, had begun to supplant psych-rock as the soundtrack of student radicalism.

FELA RALLIES HIS SUPPORTERS AFTER BEING RELEASED FROM POLICE CUSTODY IN LAGOS. MID 1970S.

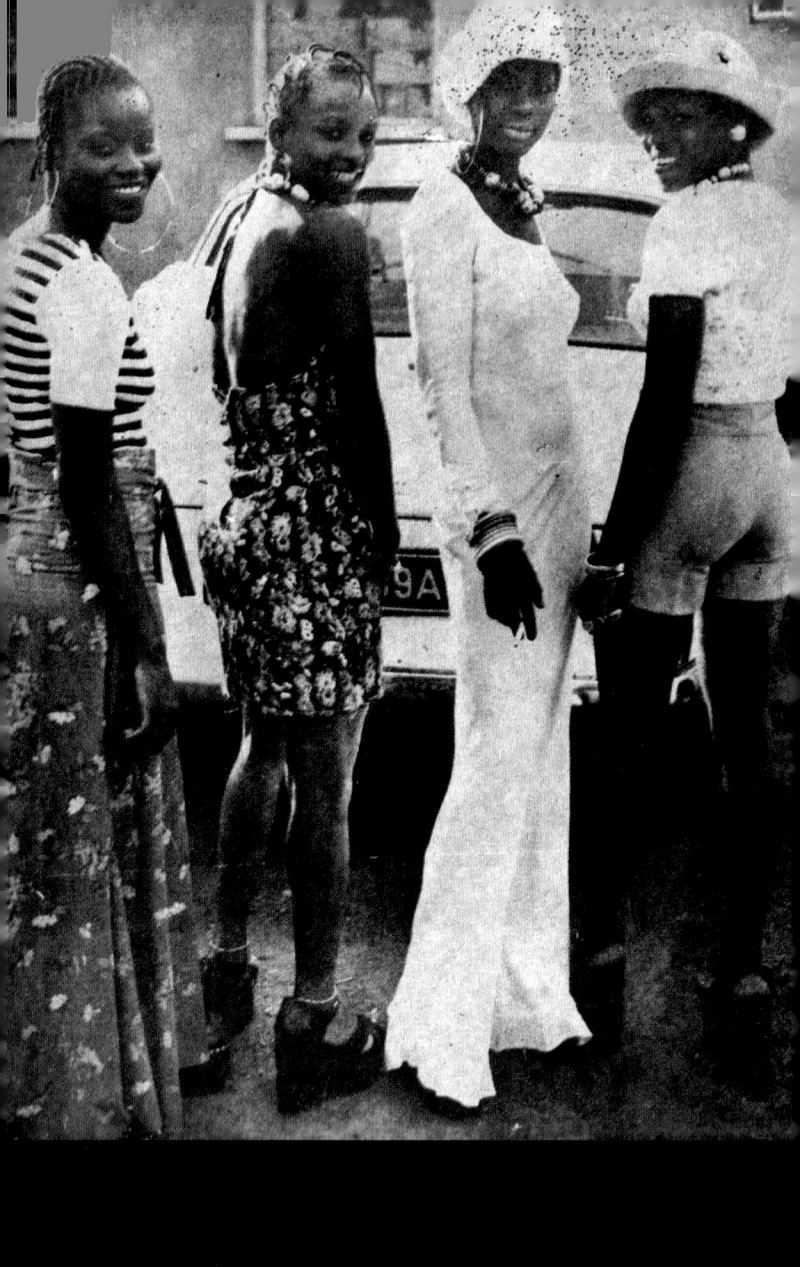

SOME OF FELA'S "QUEENS" AT THE KALAKUTA REPUBLIC, 1976

PART FIVE

THE (ROCK) WORLD ENDS

FELA KILLS THE NIGERIAN ROCK STAR

By the end of the 1970s, something – again – seemed different.

Rock and funk were still around, but the aura of coolness around their scenes had dissipated – and nobody could quite say exactly when or how it had happened. In retrospect, the first cracks probably started appearing early on, within a few years of the end of the Civil War.

Fela played a notable part in Nigerian rock's waning allure. The rise of the soul and rock scene had bestowed upon Fela a level of relevance and inspiration that he had been denied during his highlife era – recall that he and the Hykkers shared bills in Nigerian rock's earliest days. But as his popularity grew, he cannibalized the rock market's fans. Inspired by the Black pride ethos then chic in American soul and jazz, Fela increasingly fashioned his music and image around a pro-Black philosophy, fiercely advocating a celebration of traditional African values. From rock music he absorbed the more hedonistic elements of the hippie lifestyle, turning his compound into a commune marked by conspicuous displays of nudity, free love and drug use, which incited the ire of Nigeria's conservative military government. Thus, Fela became the frequent target of splashy police raids and sensational court cases that captivated the public – and won him scores of new fans, mystified by this courageous (or foolhardy) man unafraid of the soldier boys. Ever the canny self-promoter, Fela turned his clashes with the authorities into the thematic center of his art, displaying his wounds from these skirmishes like badges of honor on the sleeve art of his albums, recounting his adventures in epic detail in his lyrics and transforming himself into a modern-day folk hero, a sui generis icon of anti-authoritarianism.

The unfortunate side effect of Fela's beatification for his Afro Rock peers, however, was that they were overshadowed by this larger-than-life persona. Fela was fighting the police and the government in real life, giving voice to the frustrations many Nigerians felt about their country's heavy-handed military regime; the chronicles of his battles in the newspapers, on television and in his own music made the average rocker's outlaw image look like empty posturing. Fela was the real rebel, and so his Afro Beat sound became the real rebel soundtrack. Fela, the man who had welcomed Ginger Baker with open arms (while wearing little else) upon his arrival to Lagos, had as much foreign influence in his music as any of the Nigerian rock bands, but he had successfully branded Afro Beat as a pure and authentic African sound, the true, unfiltered voice of his African people. Afro Rock? Why, that was just a shallow imitation of millionaire Western pop stars, and was devoid of any concrete connection to the contemporary Nigerian's reality.

Another blow to rock's standing was the massive post-war upsurge of juju music. Juju had been popular in Lagos and the rest of the Yoruba Southwest since the 1930s, but it had been something of a niche taste compared to dance band highlife's broad influence in society. Highlife was glamorous and cosmopolitan, with musicians in sharp western suits and loud, glossy horn sections; its appeal was cross-ethnic, inviting fans and performers from every corner of the country to join the dance. Juju on the other hand was relatively rustic and low-impact, both sonically and visually. It featured players seated and dressed austerely in traditional attire, playing in small combos composed of a single, modestly-amplified guitar (and maybe an accordion, along with a tambourine or other hand percussion). Juju fans were mostly those who could understand its Yoruba lyrics and appreciate its Yoruba cultural references, which in the Yoruba-dominated Southwest represented a significant segment of the populace, but not one broad enough to establish it as anything more than a regional taste aimed primarily at an older, more conservative audience. What juju was not, however, was sexy or worldly.

When the highlife orchestras left Lagos during the war, it created a void that juju—and soul music—expanded to fill. From this cultural space emerged a new generation of juju stars like Sunny Ade, Ebenezer Obey and Prince Adekunle, who redirected juju with their youthful vision and embrace of new modes of

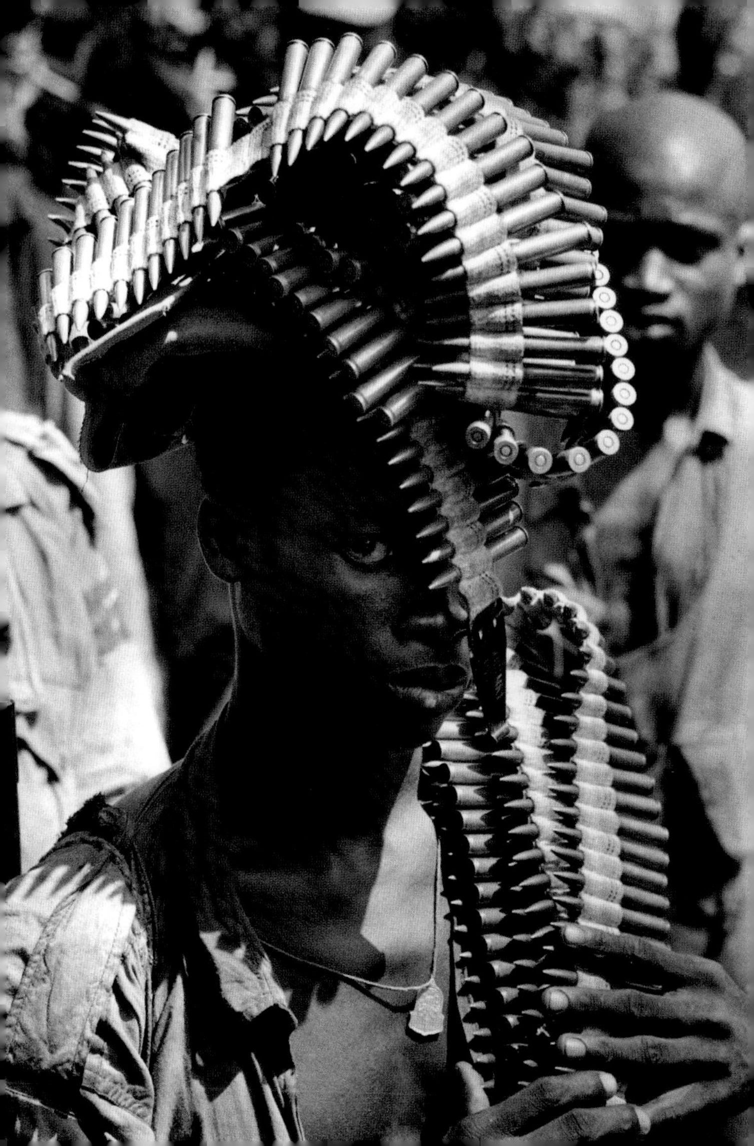

"COME BACK BABY" BY THEODORE NEMY & HIS BAND, RELEASED IN 1973.

musical expression and performance. Taking inspiration from their peers in the soul and rock scenes, the new crop of juju musicians integrated cutting-edge trappings—electronic amplification, trap drum sets, bass guitars, electric keyboards, platform shoes and other "psychedelic" fashions, scantily-clad go-go dancers—transforming juju from a provincial urban folk music to a flashy, modern pop genre. Juju became the pop style that had all the high-fidelity excitement and sex appeal of rock, but one—and this was of particular importance in the largely Fela-championed pro-African climate—that was still substantially rooted in "traditional" culture. Soon, juju was outselling both Afro Rock and Afro Beat in Nigeria by a wide margin.

Juju's ascendance to the main stage cast rock music in an even more unfavorable light among music fans and critics. Remi Akano, the entertainment columnist in the top national newsmagazine *The Spear*, embodied this turn in popular opinion. Akano started out the decade as one of the most passionate boosters of the soul and rock movement, filling his columns with giddy exhortations of the scene, rhapsodizing about each new rock release and challenging the authenticity and dedication of any fan who did not share his level of enthusiasm. By 1973, Akano was steadily increasing his coverage of juju musicians and starting to show signs of encroaching apathy towards rock, frequently writing off releases such as Theodore Nemy's "Come Back" as "childish teenybop." The rock bands of the East he ignored altogether, explaining that he found the entire "Eastern rock circuit" to be "a great bore." By 1976, Akano was reporting on juju almost exclusively, occasionally taking time out to viciously rip into what he perceived as the musical and moral vacuity of Nigerian rock and funk records. Upon the release of *Danger*, the debut LP by the Lijadu Sisters, immaculately produced by multi-instrumentalist veteran Biddy Wright, Akano wrote a review that characterized the album as "a mediocre, US-oriented funk release [that] features the sisters' strong sensual voices on one forgettable track after another with Biddy Wright's non-stop sub-Hendrix fuzz guitar solos driving nail after nail into the coffin. If Decca really want [sic] to do something with the sisters they should let them loose on some African material—as it is this album is about as welcome as 'Cliff Richard's Reggae Party'."

The album *No Stop Dis Musik* by the psychedelic funk-rock group T-Fire (led by the audacious South African guitarist Themba Matebese) provoked an even more savage mauling:

> Armed with a barrage of electronic gadgetry, a big mouth (plus an even bigger echo chamber), an armful of import albums and by the sound of it a suitcase of amphetamine cut with weed killer, Matebese is attempting to pass off his shoddily played collection of US funk clichés as something original or even desirable.
>
> ...[A] microcosm of the worst aspects of the West African scene—poorly assimilated imported styles played with high volume mania and a lack of any style or understanding. This album isn't music, it's an ugly con. And if this review sounds like psychotic raving, well, it's all it deserves. Listen to something else—listen to anything else.

While rock and funk groups continued to exist in Lagos throughout the decade, their relevance slipped. "It was hard to survive in Lagos playing rock or anything like that," says Micro Mike. "A lot of guys had to go and join juju bands." Segun Bucknor, hailed in the late 1960s as Nigeria's greatest soul star, saw the writing on the wall and in 1975 quit music to pursue a career in journalism. However, he recognized that while the pulse of rock music had gone flat in Lagos, it was still pumping east of the Niger River. "Those of us in Lagos who were still playing rock, we knew there was no market for us in most of the Southwest," Bucknor says. "But when it's time to tour, you'll see all of us heading towards the East. That's where the audience for our kind of music was. In the North, and especially in the East."

But even there the tide was slowly turning. While the Eastern rock groups stayed in business much longer than their counterparts in Lagos, they faced stiff competition from the resurging highlife scene. The Eastern highlife orchestras had been marginalized by rock during the war but, like the Lagos juju bands, they fought their way back by taking lessons from rocker style. Ditching the old-fashioned horn-dominated dance orchestra format, a new

ABOVE: (LEFT TO RIGHT) DON BRUCE WITH MEMBERS OF THE CUTES (AND LATER THE WAVES) AKUMA WALTERS AND GODDY JASPER. 1970. BELOW: THE FUNKEES' OKEREKE AND HIS GIRLFRIEND MERCY, HANGING OUT IN ABA, MID 1970S.

REVELERS AT A SOUL PARTY IN LAGOS. 1969.

generation of highlife groups organized themselves according to the rock formula—guitar-led sound, electronic amplification and sonic effects, superfly threads—and won back popular sentiment. Furthermore, the joyous, discordant, "underground" aesthetic of the early 1970s rock scene was losing ground to a more standardized commercial template. "I think as we left the violence of the war behind, people wanted to calm down," says Renny Pearl of Aktion. "They didn't want the kind of 'heavy' sound we were playing. What they wanted was a more 'sweet,' light type of music like the Apostles or the Wings." "They called it 'Ariaria music'," says Marshall Udo of Founders 15, "after Ariaria International Market in Aba, the largest open market in West Africa. This was commercial music. Not only in the sense of being the most popular style, but it was the kind of music that traders in the market liked to play in their shops to attract customers." In essence, Eastern rock had been reduced to functioning as chirpy advertising jingles.

Moreover, changes in the music economy were corroding the viability of the band model itself. As the disco phenomenon came to the fore, more and more nightclubs preferred to hire deejays over live musicians; royalties from record sales (which had been paltry to begin with) could not make up for the loss of gig revenue. "Most of the bands at this time were operating under tremendous debt," says Pearl. "The center could not hold. Most of us started to fall apart. Those who stayed playing music had to go to the studio to work as session men, but many others left music behind completely to find other ways to survive."

"But the deathblow," Pearl continues, "came when [military head of state] Olusegun Obasanjo was having his trouble with Fela. He wanted to strike at Fela's livelihood so he imposed severe taxes on the importation of musical instruments and other electronic equipment. So a pack of bass strings that we were buying for around fifty kobo [equivalent to $1.09 today] was now three naira [$3.27]. A Fender Stratocaster that had previously cost seven hundred naira [$424] is now almost three thousand naira [$6,584]. It was something Obasanjo did primarily to hurt Fela but it ended up being a blanket punishment imposed across the entire music business and it killed us all."

But despite the myriad hardships, Nigerian youth music didn't die off altogether; in fact, the 1980s would be see the music industry expand exponentially with the flowering of scores of independent labels and artists vending a range of styles from pop to highlife, disco and boogie, juju, apala, fuji, gospel, reggae and rap. A lot of it was pretty good. A bunch of it was even great.

But something was... different.

The grunge was gone, replaced by gloss. More cleanness equaled less meanness. The days of the "underground" scene were a fast-fading memory, rarely mentioned in polite company. Even the survivors of the postwar rock scene appeared eager to omit it from their resumés, avoiding association with those heady days in the same way the average Nigerian avoided discussion of the war. Rock was messy, loud, complicated and agitating... much like the war itself. But unlike the bluesy chords of a rock song, the emotions of the war had never been allowed to resolve themselves; the fighting had ended abruptly and the subsequent "no victor, no vanquished" policy had discouraged much in-depth analysis in the aftermath of the conflict.

Let sleeping dogs lie, allow the psychic wounds to scab over and heal. Today, in the second decade of the twenty-first century, those wounds still remain sensitive to the touch and continue to reopen and fester—the heightening terrorism of the extremist Islamic sect Boko Haram; the persistent efforts of a new generation of rebels to reignite the Biafra secession movement; the endless, violent tussles over which region of the country will rule them all. All of these modern conflicts can trace their origins to the war, forty-some years ago. Back in the late 1970s, barely ten years after the ceasefire, rock music and its sound of fury, chaos and confrontation evoked the baggage of violence and instability that Nigerians were trying to jettison in the effort to move forward.

Or maybe that's reading too much into it. Maybe the sound just became passé. Modern Nigerians have always been avid trend followers, and quickly grow bored, eager for the next, new thing. The 1970s saw most of the globe descending into a fuel crisis while oil-producing countries like Nigeria experienced an unprecedented economic boom. This era of prosperity and conspicuous consumption precipitated an urban preference for a glittering aesthetic that was more glamorous, with flavors smoother to the palate.

ABOVE: THE SEMI-COLON'S LASBREY OJUKWU (LEFT) IN REHEARSAL WITH SEGUN BUCKNOR (RIGHT) IN UMUAHIA. 1974. BELOW: LASBREY OJUKWU AND THE SEMI-COLON IN EMI STUDIO, LAGOS. 1975.

THE FUNKEES' OKEREKE WITH SOME AFROCENTRIC FANS. MID 1970S.

And so the rugged, dirty rock and funk of the early 1970s was discarded and left to languish, wilting away on poorly preserved reels at Decca, EMI, Clover and ARC as the foreign conglomerates' old offices were purchased, tapes buried, music lost, musicians' contact information misplaced. And an entire scene—a scene that had defined a generation—was forgotten, even by members of that generation themselves. "You know what one of my musician colleagues said?" Dele Olaseinde asked me. "He said 'What a waste of time those days were. Why did we even bother playing that music that nobody even remembers now? Where did it get us? Maybe if we had played juju, at least we would still be remembered. We wasted those years.'"

With all respect due to this regretful musician, we must disagree. While most of the artists of the Nigerian rock generation may not have achieved lasting fame or fortune, they did contribute to transforming their society. As the first generation to come of age in an independent Nigeria, they helped define the voice, the style, the zeitgeist of Nigerian-ness in the modern era. These were kids who were born in the 1940s and 1950s, into a world governed by the rigid spine and stiff upper lip of the British Empire, and its concern with politeness, protocol and the proper-thing-to-do. The freedom the rock scene gave them allowed them to let their hair down (or grow it out… or shave it off), explore different modes of expression, and use the larger culture as a laboratory in which they synthesized the modern definition of a Nigerian. That distinctive "Naija swagger" today's Nigerian hip-hop stars wield as their trademark? The confident attitude and flashy sense of style that Nigerians view as inherent cultural characteristics? None of that's anything new—but it was when the Nigerian rockers did it in the 1970s.

The visual and sonic flamboyance of modern juju music? The deep "Afro" sound of latter-day highlife? Wouldn't have happened without rock kicking in the gates of convention that had ruled Nigerian music before the war.

It might be idealistic to think that music can really change the world, but in Nigeria's case, it might have done just that. Or at least it changed people's minds, which is the first step in any revolution. Those bold rockers started a movement that continued to build and percolate through society as they themselves were forgotten along the way. But even then, they wouldn't stay forgotten long.

Over the years, the records they made have transcended the ramparts of time, geography, race, culture and language to find a new generation of acolytes across the ocean in America, Europe and Asia. And thanks largely to the curatorial work done by record labels such as this one, Soundway, Strut and Academy, we're able to view the Nigerian rock years through a historical lens and measure it up against others from around the world. On the continent, only Zambia and Zimbabwe can boast of a rock scene as intense as Nigeria's, and yet theirs—as invigorating as they may seem in their recent rediscoveries—have hardly registered the same contemporary appeal or displayed the same breadth, variety and originality that the Nigerian rock scene did. Indeed, the international regard for Nigerian rock and funk has become an institution unto itself—even enveloping some of the classic rock stars who inspired the Nigerian rockers to begin with.

"It's crazy," said Stoneface Iwuagwu of P.R.O., upon hearing the 2013 cover of his group's "Blacky Joe" by Robert Randolph & the Family Band with Carlos Santana. "Carlos Santana was everything to us back then when we were coming along. It was because of him, Eric Clapton, Jimi Hendrix that anybody picked up a guitar back then. And then today I'm listening to him singing the song I wrote? It's very humbling."

So while we would be content to provide here (for the first time, in many cases), legitimate reissue of music lost not only in the annals of Nigeria's, but the world's musical vaults, we are firmly committed to the ideas we've espoused here and the musicians who made them possible. As encapsulated in the Waves' words, the title of this anthology, it's time to wake up, you, and pay attention not just to the fuzz, funk and fury of Nigerian rock in its golden age, but its importance on Nigeria's, and the world's stage.

MEMBERS OF TONY GREY'S BLACK 7 PUT ON A SHOW, WARRI. 1975.

Recording Information/Personnel:

"Never Never Let Me Down" by Formulars Dance Band originally released in 1973 on the Afrodisia single DWA 47 "Never Never Let Me Down"/ "Adanma Hasiam." Written by Fred Alaribe. Produced by Dave Bennett. Recorded at Decca Studio, Lagos, Nigeria in 1973 by unknown engineer. Unknown personnel.

"Everybody Likes Something Good" by Ify Jerry Krusade originally released in 1972 on the Polydor single 206804POF "Everybody Likes Something Good" / "Nwantinti/Die Die." Written by Jeremiah "Ify Jerry" Jiagbogbu. Producer unknown. Recorded at Phonogram Studio, Lagos, Nigeria in 1972 by unknown engineer. Personnel: Ify Jerry (Lead Vocals, Lead Guitar); unknown remaining personnel, possibly including Benna Kemfa (Guitar), Popo Kamson (Guitar), Kingsley "King UD" Obiche (Percussion).

"Keep On Moving" by the Hygrades originally released in 1972 on the HMV single HNS 1064 "Rough Rider"/"Keep On Moving." "In The Jungle (Instrumental) by the Hygrades originally released in 1972 on the HMV single HNS 1047 "In The Jungle (Vocal)/"In The Jungle (Instrumental)". Both written by Goddy Oku. Produced by Chris Nwaiga. Recorded at EMI Studio, Lagos, Nigeria in 1972 by unknown engineer, possibly Emmanuel Odenusi. Personnel: Elvis Ato Arinze (Vocals) Goddy Oku (Lead Guitar), Clement Amaechi (Rhythm Guitar), Kevin Coburn (Bass), "Frank" (Drums).

"Stone The Flower" by the Hykkers originally released in 1972 on the HMV single HNS 1280 "God Gave His Only Son"/"Stone the Flower." Written by Jake Sollo and Jeremiah "Ify Jerry" Jiagbogbu. Produced by Odion Iruoje. Recorded at EMI Studio, Lagos, Nigeria in 1972 by unknown engineer, possibly Emmanuel Odenusi. Personnel: Pat Finn (Lead Vocals), Ify Jerry (Lead Guitar), Willie Bestman (Vocals, Percussion), Jeff Afam (Rhythm Guitar), Jake Sollo (Bass, Vocals), Emile Lawson (Drums).

"Onye Ije" by the Strangers originally released in 1972 on the HMV single HNS 1205 "Love Rock"/"Onye Ije." Written by The Strangers. Produced by Chris Nwaiga. Recorded at EMI Studio, Lagos, Nigeria in 1972 by unknown engineer, possibly Emmanuel Odenusi. Personnel: Sam Matthews (Lead Vocals), Bob Miga (Organ, Vocals), Timmy Nebuwa (Rhythm Guitar, Vocals), Anii Hofnar Umebuani (Lead Guitar), Joe Arukwe (Bass), Tammy Evans (Drums).

"Baby I Need You" by the Funkees originally released in 1973 on the HMV single EMI S 004N "Akpankoro"/"Baby I Need You." Written by Bill Ike. Produced by The Funkees. Recorded at EMI Studio, Lagos, Nigeria in 1973 by unknown engineer, possibly Emmanuel Odenusi. Personnel: Bill Ike (Lead Vocals, Electric Piano), Harry Mosco (Guitar), Danny "Heibs" Ibe (Bass, Vocals), Chyke Madu (Percussion, Vocals), Sonny Akpan (Congas), Ben Alaka (Drums).

"Mother" by Waves originally released in 1973 on the Afrodisia single DWA 62 "Wake Up You"/"Mother." Written by April Laine, Dave Kumalo, Akuma Walters and Goddy Jasper. Produced by Dave Bennett. Recorded at Decca Studio, Lagos, Nigeria in 1973 by unknown engineer. Personnel: April Laine (Lead Guitar, Lead Vocals), Dave Kumalo (Guitar, Vocals), Akuma Walters (Bass, Vocals), Eric Mann (Drums).

"Graceful Bird" by War-Head Constriction originally released in 1973 on the Afrodisia single DWA 29 "Graceful Bird"/"Shower of Stone." Written by Etim Bassey. Produced by Dave Bennett. Recorded at Decca Studio, Lagos, Nigeria in 1973 by unknown engineer. Personnel: Martin Amenechi (Guitar, Vocals), Femi Lasode (Bass, Vocals), Etim Bassey (Drums, Vocals).

"Beautiful Daddy" by Ofo the Black Company originally released in 1972 on the Afrodisia single DWAX 1 "Allah Wakbarr"/"Beautiful Daddy." Written by Larry Ifedioranma. Produced by Dave Bennett. Recorded at Decca Studio, Lagos, Nigeria in 1972 by unknown engineer. Personnel: Popo Kamson (Guitar, Vocals), Benna Kemfa (Guitar, Vocals), Larry Ifedioranma (Drums,

Vocals), Soni Makoko (Bass), Ify Jerry (Organ, Vocals), Johnny Ifedioranma (Percussion, Vocals), Kingsley Obiche (Percussion).

"Ije Udo" by the Magnificent Zeinians originally released in 1972 on the HMV single HNS 1363 "Ije Udo"/"She's My Love." Written by Tony Grey. Produced by Odion Iruoje. Recorded at EMI Studio, Lagos, Nigeria in 1974 by unknown engineer, possibly Emmanuel Odenusi. Personnel: Tony Grey (Electric Piano), Eddy Pollo Neesackey (Lead Guitar), Mac Miller (Rhythm Guitar), Maxwell Lee (Organ), Johnny Ashi (Bass), Play Parker (Drums), Rex Gildo (Percussion).

"Never Too Late" by the Apostles originally released in 1976 on the EMI album NEMI LP 0126 *The Apostles*. Written by Joel Madubuike. Produced by Chris Nwaiga. Recorded at EMI Studio, Lagos, Nigeria in 1976 by Emmanuel Odenusi. Personnel: Walton Arungwa (Lead Guitar), Chyke Fussion Okoro (Lead Vocals), Benjamin Davidson (Organ), Murphy Williams (Vocals), Harrison Mba (Rhythm Guitar), Henry Tandu (Bass), Joel Madubuike (Drums).

"Groove The Funk" by Aktion originally released in 1975 on the Clover LP CXL 2001 *Groove The Funk*. Written by Aktion. Produced by Ben Okonkwo. Recorded at EMI Studio, Lagos, Nigeria in 1975 by Kayode Salami. Personnel: Essien Akpabio (Lead Vocals), Lemmy Faith (Lead Vocals, Rhythm Guitar) Renny Pearl (Bass), Chyke Odukwe (Organ, Vocals), Ben Alaka (Drums), Abayomi Frank (Congas).

"Ballad of a Sad Young Woman" by Wrinkar Experience originally released in 1972 on the HMV single HNS 1422 "Money To Burn"/"Ballad of a Sad Young Woman." Written by Ginger Forcha Produced by Tonny Clark and Odion Iruoje. Recorded at EMI Studio, Lagos, Nigeria in 1972 by unknown engineer, possibly Emmanuel Odenusi. Personnel: Ginger Forcha (Lead Vocals, Organ, Piccolo), Edjo'o Jacques Racine (Bass, Vocals), Danie Ian (Guitars, Vocals) Collins Osokpor (Drums).

"I Can't Be Satisfied" by the Founders 15 originally released in 1972 on the HMV single EMI S 061 N "Be My Own"/"I Can't Be Satisfied." Written by Marshall Udo. Produced by Chris Nwaiga. Recorded at EMI Studio, Lagos, Nigeria in 1974 by unknown engineer, possibly Emmanuel Odenusi. Personnel: Iyke Peters (Lead Vocals), Marshall Udo (Bass, Vocals), Nek Adririka (Guitar), Sony Enang (Keyboards, Vocals), Ifeanyi Sam Akpati (Drums).

"Float" by Tirogo Originally released in 1977 on the EMI album NEMI LP 0283 *Float*. Written by Wilfred Ekanem. Produced by Emmanuel Odenusi. Arranged by Wilfred Ekanem. Recorded at EMI Studio, Lagos, Nigeria in 1977 by Monday Oki and Kayode Salami. Personnel: Wilfred Ekanem (Lead Vocals, Bass, Rhythm Guitar, Percussion), Wilfred Iwang (Drums, Vocals), Elvy Akhionbare (Lead Guitar, Percussion), Funmi Onabuolu (Keyboards, Percussion), Godwin Debogie (Conga, Percussion, Vocals).

"Scram Out" by Question Mark originally released in 1977 on the EMI album NEMI LP 0202 *Be Nice To The People*. Written by Franklin Izuora. Produced by Odion Iruoje. Arranged by Franklin Izuora. Recorded at EMI Studio, Lagos, Nigeria in 1977 by Monday Oki. Personnel: Franklin Izuora (Lead Vocals, Organ), Chyke Okafor (Drums), Victor Egbe (Lead Guitar), Uzo Agulefo (Percussion), Amechi Izuora (Bass).

"Tell Me" by P.R.O. originally released in 1976 on the EMI album NEMI LP 0177 *Blacky Joe*. Written by Justus Nnakwe, Stoneface Iwugwu & Drago Uboma. Produced by Odion Iruoje. Recorded at EMI Studio, Lagos, Nigeria in 1976 by unknown engineer, possibly Emmanuel Odenusi or Kayode Salami. Personnel: Justus "Jay U" Nnakwe (Guitar, Vocals), Stoneface Iwuagwu (Drums, Vocals), Drago Uboma (Bass, Vocals), Johnnie Woode Olimmah (Organ and Moog), Goddy Oku (Strings), Monday Oki (Percussion).

NA 5120
(p)(c) 2015 Now-Again Records.

This compilation produced by
Eothen Alapatt and Uchenna Ikonne.

Liner notes by Uchenna Ikonne,
edited by Eothen Alapatt.

Restoration and remastering by
Dave Cooley for Elysian Masters,
Los Angeles.

Production coordination by
Mark Taylor.

Cover image and select booklet images
© Gilles Caron (Contact Press Images).

Art direction by Errol F. Richardson.

Now-Again Records would like to thank:
Uchenna Ikonne, Richard "Heavyfuzz" Leckie, Miles Cleret, Greg Smith, Goddy Oku, Stoneface Iwuagwu, Justus Nnakwe, Anii Umebuani, Chike Okoro, Benjamin Davidson, Walton Arungwa, Ginger Forcha, Danian Mbaezue, Tino Martins, Richard Cole, Harry Mosco, Dele Olaseinde, Godwin Maduforo, Renny Nwosa, Marshall Udo Orru, Felix Odey, Jeremiah Jiagbogu, Pat Finn Okonjo, Lasbrey Ojukwu, Bob Agim, Tony Benson, Segun Bucknor, Maxcy Chuku, Danny Ibe, Graham Gaffney, Perry Ernest, Ephraim Nzeka, Mike Appoh, Eric Mann Chukwu, Olubamidele Amenechi, Soga Benson, Franklin Izuora, Uzo Agulefo, Wilfred Ekanem, Tony Grey, Willie Bestman, Celestin Nyam, Patrick Udoh, Prince Bola Agbana, Eyo Hogan, Charles Duke, Sylvester Akaiso, Soki Ohale, Steve Black Aiwansosa, Tony Amadi, Clifton Agwaze and Laolu Akins.

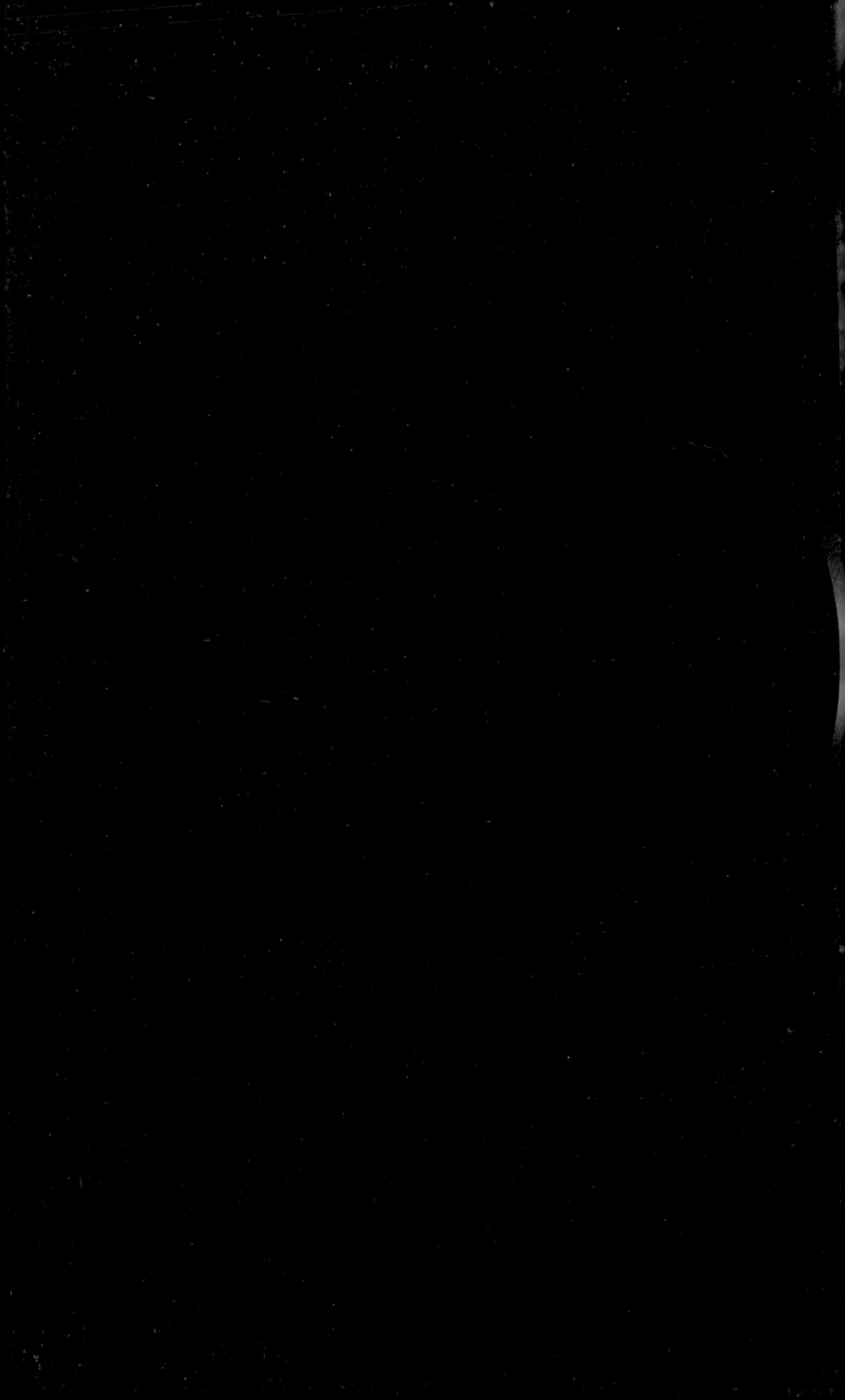